Reservation Policy in India

Policy Studies Series

The Orient BlackSwan 'Policy Studies Series' is designed to fill a visible gap in existing Social Sciences literature: the need to address, empirically investigate and rigorously analyse public policy in the field of governance.

It is important to study the policy world in its entirety because:

- Policies establish the context within which we live out our individual and collective lives and deeply impact the way we and future generations will live and work.
- Policy-making and implementation is a process that is deeply embedded in politics, and serves as an entry point into the politics of a country.
- Public administrators, scholars, journalists, and specialists need to understand the relationship between knowledge systems, technology and the making of policy, the nature of public participation and responses, and how politicians seek to forge networks to ensure that policy is transformed into law.
- Policy-making highlights the linkages between domestic and global contexts. Ideas disseminated through global institutions and civil society networks impact policy making insofar as they influence identification of problems and propose resolutions.

The literature generated through the Series, we hope, will serve to identify the strength and lacunae of the making of policy and its implementation in India.

The Series Editors

The Series Advisory Board

Reservation Policy in India

State, Social Justice, and Affirmative Action

Narender Kumar
and
Sudhir Kumar Suthar

Orient BlackSwan

RESERVATION POLICY IN INDIA: STATE, SOCIAL JUSTICE, AND AFFIRMATIVE ACTION

ORIENT BLACKSWAN PRIVATE LIMITED

Registered Office
3-6-752 Himayatnagar, Hyderabad 500 029, Telangana, India
e-mail: centraloffice@orientblackswan.com

Other Offices
Bengaluru, Chennai, Guwahati, Hyderabad,
Kolkata, Mumbai, New Delhi, Noida, Patna

First published by Orient Blackswan Private Limited 2024

ISBN 978-93-5442-645-2

042596

Typeset in
ITC Berkeley Oldstyle Std 10.5/14
by Le Studio Graphique, Gurgaon 122 001

Printed in India at
Kensington Printing & Packaging, Noida 201 301

Published by
Orient BlackSwan Private Limited
3-6-752 Himayatnagar, Hyderabad 500 029, Telangana, India
e-mail: info@orientblackswan.com

Contents

Tables

Abbreviations

AICTE	All India Council for Technical Education
BAMCEF	All India Backward and Minority Communities Employees Federation
BJP	Bharatiya Janata Party
BSP	Bahujan Samaj Party
DoPT	Department of Personnel and Training
DMK	Dravida Munnetra Kazhagam
EWS	economically weaker sections
IIM	Indian Institute of Management
IIT	Indian Institute of Technology
INC	Indian National Congress
MBC	Most Backward Classes
NCBC	National Commission for Backward Classes
NCSC	National Commission for Scheduled Castes
NCST	National Commission for Scheduled Tribes
NDA	National Democratic Alliance
OBC	Other Backward Classes
PIL	public interest litigation
PSU	public sector undertaking
PwD	Persons with Disability
RJD	Rashtriya Janata Dal
RSS	Rashtriya Swayamsevak Sangh

RTC	Round Table Conference
SC	Scheduled Caste
SP	Samajwadi Party
ST	Scheduled Tribe
UPA	United Progressive Alliance
VCC	voluntary code of conduct

Acknowledgements

Any work is a combination of opportunity, motivation, insistence, and the efforts of oneself and one's well-wishers. This volume is no exception. First of all, we would like to thank the Policy Studies series editors, who came up with a project of significance and granted us the opportunity to realise this shared vision. The contributions of Professor Sukhadeo Thorat, Professor Gopal Guru, Professor Sudha Pai, and Dr Raja Sekhar Vundru on this theme supplied us with intellectual motivation to further engage with the subject of reservation policy. We would also like to thank Gaurav Pathania, who collaborated with us on the initial conceptualisation of this book.

The decision to write the book was driven by the ongoing challenge of ensuring that the benefits of reservations accrue to marginalised social groups in India. We are thankful to our colleagues, Professor Sonajharia Minz, Dr Shailza Singh, Professor D. K. Lobiyal and Professor Surajit Majumdar who helped us understand the nuances of implementation of reservation policy in educational institutions. Special thanks are due to our colleagues at the Centre for Political Studies, Jawaharlal Nehru University who have sustained a vibrant space for discussions on social issues. Above all, this work would not have been completed without the active support of the administrative staff of the Centre for Political Studies. Last but not the least, thanks are due to the

Orient BlackSwan team, especially Roopa Sharma and Sanna Jain, who patiently facilitated work on the book despite our demanding multiple extensions.

Introduction

This book discusses one of the most stridently contested and politicised policy domains in independent India: the reservations. Although there is no clearly defined 'reservation policy', as a constitutional principle the system of reservations has shaped the nature of state policy in the country.

Public policy is defined by Cochran et al. (2003: 1) as 'an intentional course of action followed by a government institution or official for resolving an issue of public concern'. In this sense, reservations can be seen as a public policy; further, they constitute a foundational constitutional principle for the functioning of all government institutions as well as officials. The term 'reservation policy' includes various state initiatives that aim to abide by this constitutional promise. However, the gradual evolution of political mobilisation and consensus has made reservations an issue of public concern and debate in India.

We argue that the objective of reservation policy is to ensure social justice and representation of marginalised communities and groups in India. Economic objectives are just one part of these wider objectives,[1] and as a whole such policies operate within a complicated web of politics, society, and economy. Unpacking these complexities should be the objective of any policy analysis. The book therefore engages with this crucial policy domain from three interdisciplinary perspectives: history, philosophy, and politics and governance. This approach demonstrates that policies are not merely a tool for state intervention aimed at welfarism, or for achieving the distribution of economic benefits based on a cost-benefit analysis (as is widely argued in contemporary policy discourse). Reservation policy in India has largely been understood within this broad philosophical–theoretical background.

In the case of India, the political climate of any policy is defined by two major structural factors: *first*, the Constitution as providing a wider legal framework; and *second*, electoral politics and the multi-party system as a dynamic set of variables determining the implementation of any given policy. Similarly, social and economic perspectives are also determined by the historical trajectories that shape political ideas, social movements, and mobilisation at large. While the distribution of resources and economic empowerment are both crucial objectives, they are not the defining factors for governments in making policy choices. It is the interplay of the three determinants identified above—historical processes, philosophical underpinnings, and issues of politics as well as governance—that will help us understand the objectives as well as challenges of this policy.

This book also makes a conceptual distinction between reservation policy and the policy of affirmative action. The reservation policy is based on the principle of constitutionally mandated quotas. Affirmative action, on the other hand, requires representation of the marginalised communities in particular sectors but does not necessarily mandate quotas for them, thus leaving representation efforts as voluntary. The debate on reservations in India became a part of mainstream academic and political discourse, using the nomenclature of 'affirmative action' in the 2000s, when many writings appeared on the subject. The first such case was a volume by Thomas Weisskopf, *Affirmative Action in the US and India: A Comparative Perspective* (2004).

Even though the larger framework of the book is on positive discrimination, the title usually gives the impression that its focus is on affirmative action policy in India. On the contrary, Weisskopf makes a distinction in the very beginning by referring to 'affirmative action policies in the US and reservation policy in India' (2004: 1). However, a range of writings focusing on specific policy dimensions failed to make such a distinction and applied the affirmative action policy framework to Indian policies as well (for instance, see Deshpande and Yadav 2006; Deshpande and Weisskopf 2014).

In terms of positive state interventions aimed at the development of marginalised groups, specific policy action emerged in India long before the United States (US). In 1960, when US President John F. Kennedy mentioned the term 'affirmative action' in his Executive Order no. 10925, the objective was to ensure equal opportunity for people from marginalised backgrounds in government contracts and employment. By this time, India's reservation policy had already completed more than a decade. The Constitution of India, which came into effect on 26 January 1950, made special provisions for marginalised groups that are spelt out in Articles 15 (3) and (4). Article 15 provides the right to equality as a fundamental right, but Article 15 (3) makes an exception by stating:

> Nothing in this article shall prevent the State from making any special provision for women and children.

Article 15 (4) goes one step further by bringing in marginalised caste groups. This section was added by the first constitutional amendment in 1951. It reads:

> Nothing in this article or in clause (2) of Article 29 shall prevent the State from making any special provision for the advancement

> of any socially and educationally backward classes of citizens or for the Scheduled Castes and the Scheduled Tribes.

By bringing in various provisions for reservations, the Constituent Assembly ensured the representation of marginalised groups in legislative bodies and government employment.

A major question that the Constituent Assembly debated was the meaning of the word 'backwardness' as a criterion for reservation policy. On 30 November 1948, the Assembly formally debated clauses in the Constitution related to reservation. Initially, the word 'backward groups' was in use. However, many members, especially H. J. Khandekar and Ismail Saheb from Madras advocated using 'Scheduled Castes' specifically. Some members, for example K. M. Munshi, opposed this and insisted on the term 'backward', arguing that this it was a broader term that did not restrict the policy to specific castes. However, Munshi also mentioned that caste would undoubtedly be a part of what constituted backwardness. T. M. Krishnamachari, on the other hand, argued that not providing a definition for 'backward classes' would leave it open to future litigation. He argued that the assembly should specify the meaning of the term 'backward classes' instead of leaving its interpretation to the wisdom of the parliament.

In his response to this debate, B. R. Ambedkar argued that the principle that precedes other articles is the right to equality. The term 'backward' was used to create some space to ensure the representation of groups whose presence was disproportionately low in government jobs. However, he also argued that there cannot be a straightforward definition of backwardness as it would be 'rather difficult to give a dogmatic answer' (Constituent Assembly debates 1948). Ambedkar was of the view that backwardness should be defined locally by various states or levels of government.

He accepted that it would be open to litigation but also argued that all constitutions are open to litigation, and the Indian Constitution need not be an exception (ibid.).

The word 'reservation' was debated in the Constituent Assembly as a principle for organising select sectors of the newly emerging democratic state. The term 'reservation policy' was not explicitly used in the Constitution, and the practice of suffixing the word 'policy' became common only after its implementation. Once the question of implementing the reservation principle came into practice, it posed a newer set of challenges. Different institutions, actors, and states devised mechanisms to implement this principle.

Unlike in the US, where the policy of affirmative action has been debated in the context of individual rights versus community rights, in India it is embedded in the issues of social justice and equality. The Constituent Assembly debates show that the question was not so much about the impact such provisions would have on rights—rather, it was about the groups that were to be included. In fact, the apprehensions of Constitution-makers about implementation of reservation turned out to be true as the definitions of 'backward' and 'backwardness' are at the heart of the debate in India today.

Eventually, the question of reservation went beyond the constitutional principle and became a political question. The Constitution-makers had initially included a provision of 10 years to implement reservations for Schedules Castes and Tribes in legislative bodies. Such a clause was never used for administrative vacancies or state-run academic institutions. Besides, Ambedkar did not support such a cap (Bhaskar 2022). However, every time there is a debate on reservations, references are made to this 10-year clause and the alleged impact of reservations on 'efficiency' and 'merit' of government machinery. The reservation policy and its implementation opened up a new debate about the meaning of backwardness: its sociological, economic, educational, and above all, political manifestations became fertile grounds for academic discourse. Wider questions abound: How does one define backwardness? What are the parameters for its measurement and on the basis of which data? How are we to ensure the continuity and authenticity of persons defined as backward, and what kind of bureaucratic processes are required to develop a mechanism of authentication? How should one maintain records about the implementation of the reservation principle? These were some of the basic questions that needed to be settled before the implementation of the constitutional principle of reservation. Additionally, concerns of administration and governance brought reservations into the domain of policy.

In the US, this debate emerged within the context of emerging movements for the rights of African Americans. Under the leadership of Martin Luther King Jr., the issue of civil rights became a political flashpoint amidst rising tensions of the Cold War. The American government was forced to create reconciliatory mechanisms. It initiated this process by removing racial segregation policies and opening up all forms of employment opportunities, government contracts, admissions in schools and colleges, etc., regardless of race. Multiple variables like gender, ethnicity, and language were brought within the ambit of what is referred to as policy for affirmative action. The government wanted a mechanism that would open up spaces for broader representation without making it mandatory for various institutions that opposed such measurements in the name of freedom and equality. This was in part because libertarians, who had a significant presence in the US, could have seen the adoption of a quota system as a form of state interference in their independent functioning. Unlike the Indian Constitution, which formulated a more effective middle path to ensure justice and fairness for marginalised groups, the US government found a more open-ended reconciliatory mechanism than a constitutionally mandated policy like quotas or reservations.

Thus, unlike the US where affirmative action was considered a voluntary exercise without any quota or percentage, in the case of India a quota mechanism was closely intertwined with the reservation system. The quota system mandated that various departments, ministries or organisations should have a minimum number of employees who were drawn from the marginalised castes. This was considered to be a much more effective mechanism to ensure participation of marginalised caste groups.

The concerns for representation of marginalised groups in the private sector or gender-related marginalisation became a point of discussion in India only in the late twentieth century. With the implementation of the Panchayati Raj Act of 1993, reservation for women was implemented in village institutions of self-government. It is only after the turn of the millenium that women have been granted reservation in government jobs in certain states, for instance Rajasthan and Bihar.

Despite these efforts and constitutionally mandated provisions, the implementation of reservation policy has been a difficult journey. The reservation policy was largely a bureaucratic exercise until the 1980s when Dalit-Bahujan mobilisation picked up pace in north India. The emergence of Dalit-Bahujan politics and its strong electoral articulation made two major contributions: *first*, it made the issue of reservation a question of representation; and *second*, it made the representation of Dalit-Bahujan groups a political issue. The famous Bahujan Samaj Party (BSP) slogan of the 1980s, '*Jiski jitni sankhya bhaari, uski utni hissedari*' (Higher the population, higher the participation) highlighted this issue categorically. Besides, the emergence of leaders from backward classes and their specific party formations also brought the issue of representation to the political front. Leaders like Sharad Yadav, Lalu Prasad Yadav, and Mulayam Singh Yadav played a major role in making reservations a major political issue.

The emergence of a strong civil society in India in the 1990s and 2000s also played a major role in making the implementation of reservation a critical policy agenda. In the 2000s, many Dalit as well as non-Dalit organisations raised serious concerns about the prevailing conditions of social discrimination in various institutions in India. Poor implementation of reservations was seen as a major cause for such conditions. This in tandem with the emergence of Dalits as an electoral group also necessitated engagement for various political as well as civil society groups. In the case of the University of Delhi, for instance, some teachers' organisations vehemently opposed the implementation of reservations in teaching positions (Kumar 2015). However, gradually the increasing pressure of marginalised groups forced them to make a complete U-turn on this policy. Today, the same teachers' groups can be seen projecting themselves as defenders of this policy of reservation. The rise of a vocal advocacy coalition was responsible for a major shift in the political climate of the country in support of reservations.

Nevertheless, one qualitative difference clearly manifested in the emerging Dalit-Bahujan discourse. Unlike Dalit political mobilisation in which questions of representation, reservation, and caste discrimination were intertwined, among the backward classes only the first two issues gained major political traction. Issues of caste discrimination were not addressed. Consequently, in the mobilisation by backward class groups, reservations remained a demand that had more to do with welfare, distribution of benefits, and participation in state-provided public sector jobs. It was more a tool of economic development than of social upliftment.

The implementation of the Mandal Commission Report in 1990 and introduction of reservation for the Other Backward Classes (OBCs) was a major turning point in the reservation policy domain. It was the first time post-independence that the Government of India expanded the scope of the reservation principle by incorporating a population that by many estimates would form a majority of the national population.[2] The decision to implement OBC reservations came at a critical juncture. The Indian economy was going through a difficult phase. The balance of payments crisis had begun to emerge as a major economic challenge. The coalition era of electoral politics was unable to provide political stability. Amidst this, the decision to implement the recommendations of the Mandal Commission created great upheaval in the north Indian states. A large number of students and anti-reservation activists protested against this expansion, arguing that it would take away their opportunity to study in higher educational institutions. At that point, the protest was not against the specific nature of implementation but against the very idea of expansion.

It is also important to highlight that the fall of the coalition government of the National Front (led by Prime Minister V. P. Singh) was an indication of changing caste as well as communal equations across the country. This was the time when the Bharatiya Janata Party (BJP) was trying hard to consolidate its power under the leadership of Lal Krishna Advani. Within the collective grouping of Janata Dal, opinion was divided. At one end of the spectrum were leaders like Lalu Prasad Yadav of the Rashtriya Janata Dal (RJD) who were against giving any opportunity to the BJP for political expansion. However, the leadership of most other parties within Janata Dal were not averse to the idea of allying with the BJP, including the communist parties. Since most of the national parties were led by upper caste leaders (including the Indian

National Congress [INC] and communist parties), there was little to no sympathy for the cause of reservations.

Unlike the Dalits, for whom reservation in independent India was an outcome of mobilisation, there was no such mass mobilisation of the backward classes before implementation of the Mandal Commission, barring attempts by the BSP in its party literature and its work to galvanise backward classes under the umbrella of 'Bahujan', which included Scheduled Caste (SC), Scheduled Tribe (ST), OBC, and minority communities. There were electoral groups of backward communities in various states, but they did not have any significant independent organisational voice. The initial idea of the BSP was to bring together Dalits and backward classes in order to challenge the political hegemony of the upper castes. As mentioned earlier, what marked a significant difference between backward class politics and BSP politics was the issue of caste discrimination. Unlike the BSP, which demanded that backward class groups should be sensitive to the concerns of the Dalits, other backward class groups and parties in the political mainstream, like the Samajwadi Party (SP) did not want to lose their electoral support base.

Consequently, BSP emerged as a force that could mobilise Dalit votes in Uttar Pradesh (UP) on its own. It soon became a force that could not only challenge the electoral hegemony of traditionally strong parties like the Congress but also stop the backward class regional parties, as well as the BJP, from coming to power. This phenomenon culminated in the emergence of three issues, which became major political agenda for the next few decades: caste discrimination, representation of marginalised communities, and reservation policy. The BSP government in UP led by Mayawati brought in newer parameters of governance in a state that was otherwise considered poorly governed. The BSP government's proactive actions against any complaint related to caste discrimination, violence or atrocities made it an extremely popular party amongst the Dalits. It also resulted in a shift of Dalit votes from the Congress to the BSP and an almost complete disappearance of the Congress from the politics of India's most populous state (Bose 2009; Pai 2002).

A number of scholars have written extensively about this phase of Indian politics. Gail Omvedt (1994) referred to collectivisation by Dalits and farmers as the 'new farmers' movements'; Christophe Jaffrelot (2003) termed the increasing mobilisation among Dalits a 'silent revolution'. Yogendra Yadav (1999) described the increase in electoral participation among marginalised groups as 'the second democratic upsurge'. In this process, the larger phenomenon that political scientists sought to understand was the rise of Dalits as a major political force in various parts of India.

The BSP model of governance aided the electoral consolidation of Dalit votes in some other parts of India as well, sending a clear message to the other national parties like the Congress, BJP, and the communist parties that the Dalit cause was India's most urgent issue and required effective political intervention. The bureaucratisation of reservations was no longer sufficient. This political climate fuelled some major developments at the national level. The formation of three separate national commissions—for SC, ST, and OBC groups—was also an outcome of this process. However, there was little discussion about the policy-level changes that emerged through this new politics. Although the issue of reservation was debated amid the implementation of Mandal Commission recommendations, the focus was not on how to make it effective. Instead, the debate was on whether the reservation policy was required at all, the question of 'merit', and how long the policy should continue. Thus, at a time when major changes in policy were taking place at the macro level, social scientists were still debating older questions. The critique of this idea of 'merit' and 'quality' has only recently gained wider traction, with anti-caste scholars arguing that placing merit and reservations on opposite sides creates a false binary.[3]

Amidst this academic negligence and changing political scenario, three major macro level policy changes occurred at the national level. *First*, the government started special drives to fulfil various reserved positions which were either lying vacant or were not utilised at all. *Second*, autonomous bodies like universities and public sector undertakings (PSUs) were given clear instructions to fill up reserved positions. *Third,* the earlier logic of merit and quality was done away with to prioritise wider concerns of representation and social justice.

This also resulted in newer studies regarding issues of efficiency and its impact on reservations, and the need to implement reservation in the private sector, etc. The *Economic and Political Weekly* published a series of articles concerning the principles of reservation and crucial policy concerns. Surinder S. Jodhka (Jodhka and Newman 2007; Mahajan and Jodhka 2010) and Satish Deshpande (Deshpande and Yadav 2006) attempted to understand the question of caste discrimination in this context. Ashwini Deshpande (Deshpande and Weisskopf 2014) on the other hand looked at the idea of efficiency and its relationship with the question of reservations. Sukhadeo Thorat wrote extensively on the policy of reservations (2005, 2007), especially its economic aspects and the case for private sector reservations.

A significant outcome of this was the Eleventh Five-Year Plan (2007–2012) which had a special emphasis on social inclusion. The focus of the Plan was on development for marginalised sections of society, including Dalits, Adivasi communities, backward classes, women, and minority groups. The budgetary allocation for special component plans in each ministry or department became a major issue and was extensively discussed at this time. The union government also announced gender budgeting as part of its policy monitoring mechanism. Besides, special drives were carried out to implement the Mandal Commission Report.

The National Commission for Scheduled Castes (NCSC) played a major role in highlighting major policy gaps at various levels. Their reports provided an exhaustive account of implementation of reservation policy. The commission not only highlighted concerns for reservation for the SCs but also brought in larger perspectives on other marginalised groups. Later, the formation of the National Commission for Scheduled Tribes (NCST) also contributed immensely to this process.

This book is divided into an introduction, four chapters, and a conclusion. Chapter 1 deals with the philosophy of reservation and the initial reservation policy as implemented in various provinces. It also examines early understandings of the policy. Chapter 2 engages with the evolution of reservation policy in India. This chapter divides the issue into two parts, extension and expansion, with the notion of 'expansion' further divided into horizontal and vertical sub-categories. This chapter also discusses various commissions, their recommendations, and emerging issues from their reports—the demands by backward classes, arguments about reservation for women, and implementation of the Panchayati Raj Act. Chapter 3 addresses issues related to micro-level policy implementation. Situating the debate on reservation in an exclusion–discrimination continuum, this chapter shows how various institutions have played a major role in the evolution of effective policy intervention methods. Further, it looks at various loopholes in the process of implementation of reservations, including gaps within institutions. Chapter 4 analyses the development of reservation policy vis-à-vis the opening up of the Indian economy in the early 1990s. The changing nature of class composition in India with its distinct caste character was responsible for emerging demands to initiate changes in the reservation policy. This chapter also elaborates on the emergence of the 'new middle classes' and an ongoing debate on reservations in the private sector. The implementation of reservation for the economically weaker sections (EWS) is also discussed within this wider context of a changing socio-economic social structure. Finally, the Conclusion discusses future pathways and methods to ensure effective, efficient, and inclusive formulation and implementation of the reservation policy.

Notes

1. For instance, see Weisskopf (2004) and Deshpande and Weisskopf (2014), which use an economic framework to understand the impact of reservations.
2. For instance, *The Indian Express* cited government data from 2018–19 to report that about half of all rural households belong to the OBC category. See Sharma (2021).
3. For instance, see Subramanium (2019).

one

The Context and Philosophy of Reservations in India

A social policy is a product of its context, that is, the socioeconomic and political conditions prevalent at the time it takes concrete shape as a set of programmes, legal codes, and implementation measures. This context determines the philosophy of the policy, and therefore the underlying philosophy may undergo transformations over time. Reservations in India are a system of varied policy measures that aim at the upliftment of socially and educationally backward citizens or groups by providing scholarships, fee concessions, reserved seats in jobs and/or educational institutions, relaxation in qualifications, etc. 'Reservation polices' designate 'the reserving of a certain number of seats or positions, in a desirable institution or occupation, for members of groups that were under-represented in such positions' (Weisskopf 2004: 4). Thus, it is a process to reduce the extent of under-representation of disadvantaged communities, involving an effort to discriminate in favour of such groups to execute measures as a part of 'compensatory discrimination' or 'protective discrimination'. There are debates about whether 'affirmative action' accurately describes the conceptualisation behind this policy in the Indian context, or whether it should be called 'protective discrimination', 'positive discrimination based on reservations' or 'quotas' (Chandhoke 2008).

Reservation policy is an effort to address various forms of exclusion, discrimination, and marginalisation based on social identity. Caste-based identity is central to these efforts. In other words, reservations in India have been intrinsically linked with, but not confined to, the question of caste. The markers of identity-based benefits under reservations have shifted over time: non-Brahmins, Backward Classes, Untouchables, Depressed Classes, Scheduled Castes, Scheduled Tribes, Other Backward Classes, etc. The categories to be covered under the policy of reservations have also evolved over the past seven decades. The most recent insertion is the category of 'economically weaker sections' (EWS) that claims to give priority to reservations on an economic basis and not on the basis of social identity.

The growth of political consciousness about caste-based identities and state intervention on their basis is not a very old phenomenon. This political churn began in limited regions of India that had witnessed the emergence of various social reforms movements in the late-eighteenth and nineteenth centuries. Various provinces in India made interventions at this time to achieve a more equitable society and ensure equal opportunities for marginalised sections. The question of access to education and employment was at the core of these efforts.

Reservations and Early Initiatives for Education of the Marginalised

Among the most prominent anti-caste reformers in the nineteenth century were Jotiba Phule and Savitribai Phule, who focused on teaching the so-called Untouchables, opposed child marriage, and supported widow remarriages. People from caste Hindu backgrounds mistreated those that they deemed 'low caste' and practised untouchability with people from other castes they considered 'impure' and 'low'. Criticism of Brahmin domination began due to the formation of non-Brahmin institutions and organisations.

Demands were raised for reservations in the years 1882 in Pune and 1891 in Travancore. In 1902, Rajarshi Shahu, the Maharaja of the princely state of Kolhapur, made provisions for non-Brahmin and backward classes by providing reservations to them in education and administration. He opened hostels for students and imparted free education to all without any discrimination (Vundru 2003; Weisskopf 2004). Further, the kind of education his government imparted was aimed at ensuring that students were gainfully employed. Shahu opposed untouchability and advocated for a class-free society. He provided 50 per cent reservation to the backward classes (Weisskopf 2004: 10–11). In 1918, Nalvadi Krishnaraja Wadiyar, Raja of Mysore formed a committee to implement measures for non-Brahmins, giving them reservations in employment and education (ibid.). The princely state of Mysore considered all groups other than Brahmins as 'backward classes' and reserved quotas for them in colleges and state services. This was a first in the Indian subcontinent. In Madras Presidency, the Communal Government Order (G. O. 613), which was passed on 16 September 1921, was again an unprecedented step in favour of reservations by the Justice Party government (ibid.). Specific quotas were assigned in public appointments in 1926. As per these quotas, for every 15 appointments, two were granted to Brahmins, two to 'backward', that is, low-caste Hindus, six to other Hindus, two to 'depressed', that is, untouchable castes, two to Anglo-Indians and Christians, and one to a Muslim (Vundru 2003; Weisskopf 2004: 10–11). Similarly, Bombay Presidency instituted a reservation policy in the year 1925. These reservations set an example of inclusivity for future policy-making.

Prior to the emergence of these social reform movements and interventions by princely states, education was considered a special prerogative of the 'higher strata' of society, especially the first three varnas. Further, each of the three had its own traditional specialisation: formal teaching among Brahmins; martial training among Kshatriyas; and accounts and commerce among Vaishyas. This system contributed to the maintenance of the caste system to a great extent. With the expansion of the British rule and the adoption of a Western system of education, the doors of schools and colleges were theoretically thrown open for all castes in British India, but the historical dominance of certain castes continued to cast a shadow on these efforts.

It was for this reason that Briggs observed, 'both teachers and pupils make it most difficult for lower caste boys to sit in the classrooms' (Sinha 1986: 13). The Woods Despatch of 1854 drew the colonial government's attention to the negligence of educational development among the masses. It also pointed to the Dharwar case, where a so-called untouchable boy was refused admission so that caste Hindus did not get alienated from attending the school. The discourse surrounding the case may be considered the beginning of the debate on reservations. The Court of Directors, hearing the case in 1856, observed that 'all schools maintained at the sole cost of the Government shall be open to all classes of its subjects without distinction'. The government of Bombay in 1856 declared that students would not be discriminated against on the basis of caste and race by schools, otherwise such schools would be liable to face serious action (Galanter 1984: 20–21). At the individual/private level, Mahatma Phule had opened schools for the *Shudr-atishudra* in 1848. He famously wrote in

Shetkaryaca Asud (1881): 'Without education, wisdom was lost; without wisdom, morals were lost; without morals, development was lost; without development, wealth was lost; without wealth, the Shudras were ruined; so much happened through lack of education' (Ambedkar.org). This idea about the consequences of lack of education among non-Brahmins proved deeply influential among the non-Brahmin rulers and prompted them to look towards the education of these classes. The Maharaja of Baroda Sayajirao Gaekwad started schools as part of state efforts in 1883. He had to depend on Muslim teachers to run these schools as caste Hindu teachers would not accept jobs in such schools (Keer 1990: 4). Taking forward the order of Court of Directors, in 1885 Richard Temple, the Governor of Bombay proposed to reserve 50 per cent scholarship for Muslims and backward-class Hindus, realising that scholarships solely based on the criterion of merit were further perpetuating Brahmin monopoly on the overall educational system (Jain 1990). Mahatma Phule's efforts had a decisive impact on Shahuji Maharaj of Kolhapur and in 1917 he pioneered free and compulsory primary education for non-Brahmins including Dalits. Realising the dire need to make education possible for the most marginalised, he passed a Hujur Order—a kind of state policy order—which stated that

> any Untouchable student joining any state aided or helped educational institution should be treated respectfully like a gentleman and taken into school rooms. If any man in the state education staff has any objection to his doing so, he must send in his resignation within six weeks from the receipt of this order. (Vundru 2003: 72)

The relatively privileged non-Brahmin castes were realising their absence from important positions of power in society. Even though some of the rulers of various regions came from the non-Brahmin castes, influential positions of governance were primarily held by Brahmins. In the colonial government, the Brahmins held around 65 per cent of gazetted posts and 70 per cent of non-gazetted posts in the beginning of the twentieth century (Dushkin 1979: 662). With this realisation, some regional rulers initiated efforts to take education to the masses, especially the non-Brahmins, as discussed above. Around this time, people started organising social movements. In south India, these movements flourished greatly and effectively reduced the power of the Brahmins. The anti-Brahmin movements emphasised the need for reservations for non-Brahmins, since there were very few non-Brahmins in elite positions in the civil services and related professions for Indians in British rule. Through these movements, people raised their voices against unequal social dynamics, demanded reservations in government services, and also secured aid to non-Brahmins in educational institutions. These anti-Brahmin movements were variously led by communities belonging to the non-Brahmin upper castes, ethnic and religious minorities, and Dalits. Later, the term 'Depressed Classes' came into use to refer to tribal and Dalit communities (Weisskopf 2004:10).

Ambedkar and Equal Opportunity Policy against Historical Injustices

Colonial-era Policy

As the doors of formal education opened up for the backward classes and Untouchables in the princely states and colonial India, there were new possibilities of assertion among these groups. In 1917, B. R. Ambedkar returned to India and in January 1919 presented a memorandum to the Southborough Committee, which was tasked with enlarging the representation of Indians in legislative bodies. For the first time, Ambedkar formally represented the case of the Untouchables. This coincided with the period when provinces in western and southern India were earmarking space for marginalised groups in education and state services.

Ambedkar made a systematic argument to the Southborough Committee for remedies against caste discrimination and to reform the representation system outlined in the Government of India Act, 1919. After about 10 years, an attempt was made once again to revise the 1919 Act, this time through a series of Round Table Conferences (RTCs). Ambedkar submitted two statements to the Simon Commission in May 1928–1929. During the RTCs, he made various interventions through memoranda and personal presentations in the conference. However, it was only in the 1940s that the reservation policy took definite shape as it exists today. The full-fledged policy emerged even later, at the time of framing of India's Constitution in 1947, and in fact spelt out a broader concern to institute safeguards for the marginalised rather than limiting its purview merely to the reservation policy. These statements and interventions provide insights into the evolution of the reservation policy for the Scheduled Castes. These documents are fundamental to understanding the malady of Hindu society and the remedies proposed by Ambedkar to combat the denial of equal opportunity and incessant discrimination.

To set the tone, the primary challenge before Ambedkar was to establish how the Dalits were a distinct community—this went against the popular belief that they were a part of the larger caste Hindu identity. He began by arguing that just as distinctions are made among Hindus, Muslims, Parsis, Christians, etc., on religious grounds, caste divides Hindus into 'low caste' and 'high caste', and further into caste Hindus and 'Untouchables'. Ambedkar highlighted that in order to be a community, common aims, beliefs, and customs are important, but in the case of Untouchables and caste Hindus, such commonalities were completely missing. He further remarked that although non-Brahmins also struggled against the idea that Brahmins were intellectually superior, their 'theological bias prevented them from serving under low-caste officers' (Ambedkar 1979, vol. 1: 262). Hitting at the fundamental problem of religious and caste bias, he argued that 'as the Pope cannot pass a law against the teachings of Christ and a Sultan strictures against Islam similarly a Hindu cannot pass a law abolishing untouchability against his religious beliefs' (ibid.: 247–277). After 10 years of advocating for the Depressed Classes, Ambedkar observed:

> The Depressed Classes cannot be employed in the army, navy and the police because such employment is opposed to the religious notions of the majority. They cannot be admitted in schools because their entry is opposed to the religious notions of the majority. They cannot avail themselves of government dispensaries, because [*sic*] will not let them cause pollution to their person's or to their dispensaries. They cannot live a cleaner and higher life, because to live above their prescribed station is opposed to the religious notions of the majority. So rigorous is the enforcement of the Social Code against the DCs that any attempt on the part of the Depressed Classes to exercise their elementary rights of citizenship only ends in provoking the majority, to practice the worst form of social tyranny known to history. (Ambedkar 1982, vol. 2: 445)

He advocated solving the problems by (i) instituting a Compulsory Primary Education Act to enable access and inspire the Depressed Classes to avail of education; (ii) making primary education a strictly-enforced state obligation; and (iii) securing entry of the Depressed Classes in the public services to garner greater interest in education (ibid.: 427–428).

Regarding Public Services (Ambedkar 1982, vol. 2: 393–399), Ambedkar argued before the Simon Commission that the

Untouchables had essentially been excluded from public services by Brahmins who opposed their inclusion on the grounds of 'efficiency'. Invoking Gopal Krishna Gokhale's case for Indianisation of administration, which was meant to institute a preference for Indians over Europeans, Ambedkar argued that such a demand was based on good, not efficient, administration. Further, this logic held true in the case of non-Brahmins and Brahmins as well. For Ambedkar, democracy would thrive not simply on efficient governance but also good governance and representation of various groups in the administration was a mandatory condition for that. Recognising the continuing struggles for equality—between Brahmins and non-Brahmins, Hindus and Muslims, caste Hindus and Untouchables—a non-representative administration was bound to have problems of partisanship. These ill effects could only be avoided through the mandatory expansion of administration to include diverse social groups.

The next phase of Ambedkar's efforts took shape at the proceedings of the RTCs held between 1930 and 1933. This phase is marked by two major developments: (i) after nomination to the RTC, Ambedkar's vision expanded from Bombay Presidency to the all-India level, and (ii) the concerns broadened both in terms of issues and remedies (moving beyond political representation to reservations in government jobs, educational benefits, etc., and how those could be better implemented by making the Depressed Classes category in official positions). About the British government, Ambedkar commented that despite their formal efforts, 'what we do find is that they are quite incompetent to tackle our problems' (Ambedkar 1982, vol. 2: 504). He asserted that though the problems of Depressed Classes were rooted in social mechanism, these required political, not social, solutions.

There certainly was a qualitative change in Ambedkar's arguments during this period compared to the Southborough

Committee and the Simon Commission interventions. The British government looked at all minorities uniformly but Ambedkar asserted that the social status of each minority group was different. Although he agreed that minorities shared many common concerns, he felt that untouchability and social ostracism distinguished oppressed castes from other minorities.

Ambedkar and Rao Bahadur Srinivasan (a Depressed Classes leader from Madras) jointly made the first systematic representation of problems of the Depressed Classes and proposed a set of solutions comprising equal rights, legal safeguards against discrimination or violation of these rights, and a mechanism to ensure equal share and participation in public life, that is, representation in services and legislatures. They declared that without such provisions the future Constitution of India would be incomplete (Ambedkar 1982, vol. 2: 546). Emphasising that the mere provision of equal rights could not be sufficient, Ambedkar and Srinivas suggested that there was 'a need to have adequate pains and penalties from interference in the enjoyment of declared rights' in order to secure equality. Their proposal recognised that even a mere demand of equal rights could trigger a backlash; social boycott worked as an effective weapon against vulnerable groups, leading to complete alienation or segregation, and even violence (ibid.: 548–550).

The second RTC witnessed an extremely contentious discussion between M. K. Gandhi and Ambedkar that finally culminated in the Poona Pact of 1932. The Poona Pact brought to light some serious disagreements on the reservation of seats for the Depressed Classes. Instead of creating a separate electorate for the Depressed Classes, the principle of joint electorates was applied to reserve seats for Depressed Classes candidates within the Hindu electorate. Thus, all the registered voters of the constituency would vote to elect a Depressed Classes candidate. The number of seats reserved for the Depressed Classes under the Poona Pact was practically double the number reserved under the Communal Award of 1932.[1] They were not to be discriminated against in public services appointments. However, there was no fixed percentage of seats for them at this juncture. Additionally, provinces were to earmark adequate educational grants to provide facilities for members of the Depressed Classes (Ambedkar 1990, vol. 9: 85–88).

The second Round Table Conference and its culmination in the Poona Pact had a decisive impact on Ambedkar's later strategies to safeguard Dalit interests. On 4 February 1940, he openly criticised the Pact, stating that 'Safeguards under [the] Poona pact are inadequate'. After a gap of two years, Ambedkar again raised the issue of comprehensively safeguarding the interests of the Depressed Classes. He submitted a memorandum to the Governor General on 29 November 1942 in his capacity as member of the Executive Council (Ambedkar 1991, vol. 10: 405–442).

The Memorandum to the Cripps Mission was divided into four parts where the first dealt with political grievances, the second with educational grievances, the third with absence of publicity and role in government contacts, and the fourth with the duty of the government towards Depressed Classes. Interestingly, among the four political grievances, two were about lack of representation in the public services and absence of Depressed Classes in the Federal Public Services Commission as well as inadequate representation in the Central Legislature and Executive. He argued that European officials were blissfully ignorant about the need for special protections for Depressed Classes; Muslim officials strived to strengthen their position; and Hindus' self-interest combined with age-old prejudices ensured that the Depressed Classes were almost absent from public institutions. Ambedkar pointed out that the public services were a vital avenue for employment for Depressed Classes since caste-ordained practices that prohibited the adoption of new occupations effectively blocked all other opportunities. He also contended that in modern times, the administration had not only executive but also legislative power; in the hostile, unjust, and prejudiced public services, the need for representation of Depressed Classes becomes significant and compulsory. Accordingly, an order was issued in 1943 to reserve 8.33 per cent of jobs in the central government services for members of the Depressed Classes (Ambedkar 1990, vol. 10: 475).

Ambedkar expressed his views on education at various points, for instance while intervening in the discourse surrounding the Simon Commission. Here, the emphasis was more on solutions than on delineating the evolution of educational policy of the British in India and its neglect of the Depressed Classes. Education was given greater importance than even ministerial posts, as educational safeguards would positively impact a much greater population. Ambedkar advocated greater access to higher education in the field of science and technology than elsewhere.

Independence and Reservation Policy

The next phase of discourse on reservation policy involves the Constituent Assembly, wherein there was a positive view for adopting safeguards or other policy measures, including reservations, for the upliftment of marginalised sections of society, and specifically for Scheduled Castes and Scheduled Tribes. An agreement about these issues emerged in the very beginning of the Constituent Assembly meetings. On the question of reservations in public services, the wisdom of the Constituent Assembly was in favour of some safeguards for the SCs. Summarising the opinion of the House, Ambedkar made two observations: (i) that there will be equality of opportunity for all citizens and, (ii) simultaneously there will be a provision for certain communities which have so far been outside the administrative apparatus. Article 16 in the present Constitution balanced both these views (Saxena 1981: 386–388). A consensus was formed that minority groups would not press for separate electorates, and the majority community would not oppose reservation of seats for the minorities. Moreover, it was decided with the consent of Muslims and Christian representatives in the Advisory Committee that these two communities would not be treated as minorities for the purpose of representation in administration (ibid.: 391). After extensive debate and deliberation, the word 'backward' instead of minorities was used in Article 16 and specific entitlements of the SC/ST communities were provided in Article 335 regarding appointment to public services. Moreover, as stated in Article 340 of the Constitution, it was left to the government to make provisions for other backward communities which may have been left out of the policy. On the political front, a fixed proportion of seats were reserved for SC/ST candidates in both Parliament and the state assemblies (Articles 330 and 332).

A distinction was made between backward communities and Scheduled Castes and Tribes on the basis of the nature of historical injustice they had faced. The Scheduled Castes and Tribes faced a different kind of discrimination in India and were seen as being outside the so-called 'mainstream' of varna society. The way of life based on the varna system, as defined in Sanskrit-Vedic texts, was criticised by Ambedkar for creating an unequal and unjust society. Though all working communities, including cultivators, farmers, labourers, pastoralists, forest dwelling groups, etc., were considered to be at the lower rungs of the social hierarchy,

SCs and STs faced double discrimination, since in ritual terms they were placed outside varna society altogether. Dalits were treated as 'Untouchable' by both backward communities and the upper castes. Similarly, STs were considered outside the 'civilised Sanskritised way' of life even by backward classes and the SCs. In other words, there was a rigid compartmentalisation of Indian society based on caste, religion, and a narrow understanding of the 'mainstream' groups. The Constituent Assembly accepted Ambedkar's argument that this division was fundamentally based on principles of inequality and injustice.

A democratic society cannot be achieved without questioning foundational principles of society. Policy interventions such as reservations were considered one crucial step in this direction. However, reservations were not meant to replace the state's obligations to come up with legal provisions and other necessary steps for building a more equitable society. Provisions for the backward classes were an indicator of the Constituent Assembly's commitment to address backwardness in India as it manifested along the lines of identity.

Hence, the debate on reservations has also been about bringing in economic backwardness as a criterion along with social backwardness. As Chapter 2 will discuss, the logic of vertical and horizontal expansion of reservation includes these arguments. Insertion of provisions for the 'creamy layer' in reservations for backward classes is related to this. However, the most drastic policy decision in this case was introduction of reservation for the economically weaker sections (EWS). Unlike earlier policies where social and economic backwardness was considered together, in the case of EWS, the social logic was completely done away with in favour of using economic backwardness as the sole criterion for reservations.

Debates on the Category of Economically Weaker Sections (EWS)

The 103rd Constitutional Amendment introduced the quota for Economically Weaker Sections, granting reserved status on economic basis to those other than the already existing social and economic categories like SC, ST, and OBCs. This amendment gives power to the state to make provisions for the reservation of appointments or posts in favour of any economically weaker section of citizensother than SC, ST, and OBCs.

Prior to 103rd Constitutional Amendment, the EWS category had been implemented for students seeking admission in private schools in Delhi. As per the Delhi government's notification, 25 per cent seats were reserved for the EWS category, of which 22 per cent seats were allocated to disadvantaged groups: SC, ST, and OBC (non-creamy layer) students; children with disability as defined in the Persons with Disabilities Act, 1995; orphans, as defined in the Juvenile Justice Act, 2015; transgender children; and children living with or affected by HIV.[2] Thus the scope of EWS was very broad. The introduction of EWS reservations by the union government in 2019 has renewed the debate around this issue.

After the Government of India passed the 103rd Constitutional Amendment Act, two parties with very different stances filed petitions against the new category in the Supreme Court. On the one hand was the organisation Youth for Equality and on the other were various backward classes welfare groups. The former opposed caste-based policies as a whole and challenged the proposed amendment on the ground that it violated earlier rulings by the apex court that placed a 50 per cent ceiling on reservations. While the group fully supported EWS reservations, it wanted them to be implemented by converting the existing 27 per cent OBC quota into a non-caste-based economic quota, staying within the apex court's 50 per cent cap. On the other hand, leaders of backward classes welfare groups challenged reservations for EWS groups specifically, arguing that EWS groups did not fit the reservations requirements laid down by the Supreme Court in a previous case (*The Indian Express* 2023). Although the Supreme Court rejected their plea to suspend the General-Economically Weaker Sections (GEN-EWS) category's 10 per cent reservation in government positions and educational institutions, the matter was referred to a 5-member bench.

Summing Up

The debates about social identity and economic criteria as the basis for reservation policy are not merely about contestations over defining beneficiaries. They have a political context that must be given due attention in order to understand contestations around the demands for expansion and inclusion of reservations. Over the second half of the nineteenth century and early twentieth century, colonial India witnessed initiatives for the upliftment of various marginalised groups. By the end of the twentieth century and in the early 2000s, as the implementation of the policy for reservations became effective, it created groups who were its beneficiaries and those who considered themselves as having 'lost out'. This resulted in a kind of policy collision between beneficiaries and opponents of the policy.

An interesting political shift with regard to reservations is that those who were vehement opponents of the policy till the late twentieth century began to demand beneficiary status for themselves. Mass political mobilisation developed around this time, especially among the farming communities. Prominent among these are dominant caste communities that continue to demand inclusion in the face of economic precarity. However, social identity-based aspects of deprivation remained the primary criterion for reservations until the implementation of the category of EWS. The next chapter discusses the expansion of the policy of reservations and its context.

Note

1. See https://www.constitutionofindia.net/historical-constitution/poona-pact-1932-b-r-ambedkar-and-m-k-gandhi/ (accessed August 2024) for the full text of the Poona Pact, including the number of reserved seats.

2. See Circular no. DE. 15(22)/PSB/2021-22/1528–1533, dated 6 April 2021, Government of National Capital Territory (NCT) of Delhi, Directorate Of Education (Private School Branch). Old Sectt.: Delhi–110054.

two

Debates on Extension and Expansion of Reservations

Introduction

In Chapter 1, we understood the context in which the policy of reservations was initiated and its underlying philosophy. The policy has moved in different directions even as it remained focused on social and educational deprivation, with the introduction of an economic dimension at a later stage, first in terms of the 'creamy layer' in OBC reservations and then in a focused manner with the creation of an EWS category, even as other characteristics of the reservation policy continued. In this chapter we shall look at the extension and expansion of the policy, and in some ways we shall see how reservation becomes a less contested word in popular discourse. This is a significant shift—till recently, the term was deeply stigmatised as the policy was seen to be associated with the Dalits. Such attitudes reflect the persistence of caste ideology in contemporary India.

The constitutional provision of reservations for the Scheduled Castes and Scheduled Tribes had a definite impact on their socioeconomic and political upliftment. Consequently, the status of people in these categories began to improve (Srinivas 2016). Observing these developments, there was a surge in enthusiasm for reservations among other castes, communities, and groups who considered themselves to be socially, educationally, and economically weak (ibid.). Although systems of reservation for some groups other than SCs and STs were implemented in some states, there was no such provision at the level of the central government. These castes were accounted for in the broader category of 'Other Backward Classes' (OBCs) and some were listed in the category as per their social and economic status in their respective states.

The terms 'extension' and 'expansion' are generally used interchangeably, but conceptually they have slightly different meanings. Extension refers to stretching out or a lengthening process, whereas expansion indicates towards spreading out or enlargement. Thus, extension is more in terms of time and expansion in terms of people so far as policy is concerned. In the early phase discussed in Chapter 1, when non-Brahmin as a category was provided reservation by the rulers of Indian princely states, there was little sense of any extension or expansion as the orders were in themselves broad, that is, they were not time-specific and were applicable to the whole population except Brahmins. It was in the nascent stages of the formalised reservation policy under British rule that there were debates around both extension and expansion.

In 1906, as the British government formulated a set of electoral reforms, Agha Khan led a contingent of prominent Muslims and demanded separate representation in order to address their concerns about under-representation. In 1909, this demand was met in the form of separate electorates, which may be considered as a kind of reservation in the political sphere or, to be more specific, in the electoral process. In 1919 under the Government of India Act, separate electorates were extended to Sikhs, Indian Christians, Anglo-Indians and Europeans primarily on the basis of their minority status in the Indian population.

This system remained in 1929, and was in fact operational till 1947. And here came the intervention of B. R. Ambedkar, who advocated granting these measures to the Depressed Classes both in 1919 and 1929. Thus, expansion and extension were routinely discussed in this initial phase of pan-India reservations through different legislative acts.

In the decades that followed, the extension of SC/ST reservation became a point of contradiction and paradox. In popular understanding, political reservations in central and state legislatures on the one hand, and administrative reservations in educational institutions and public-sector jobs on the other are conflated with one another so far as extension (in terms of time-frame) is concerned. There was serious debate about these issues in the Constituent Assembly which culminated in Article 334, which states that political reservation would be for a period of 10 years that could be extended. In practice, this reservation has extended beyond 50 years with successive constitutional amendments in the last few decades. As mentioned in the Introduction, there was no time limit on reservations in education and public employment. The conditions of these sections of society remain precarious, so it was felt that extension of political reservation and continuation of education and employment quotas were both necessary.

Horizontal Expansion

Since the Schedules drawn up at the time of independence may require modifications to correct errors or reflect changing social dynamics, Articles 341 and 342 were introduced in the Indian Constitution. These Acts empower the President and the Parliament of India to modify the existing Schedules by including/excluding any castes, races, tribes, or even parts or sub-groups within them, which would for the purposes of the Constitution be deemed to be SC or ST in relation to a state or union territory. While for the Scheduled Castes list, this could be a caste, racial group, or tribe, the Scheduled Tribes list is restricted to tribal communities only. Accordingly these inclusions or, rarely, exclusions do take place. A major policy decision was taken in 1956 to include Dalit Sikhs within the ambit of reservations. Similarly, in 1990, Dalits who converted to Buddhism were also included in the Schedule. It is important to note that there is no religious bar in the case of the Scheduled Tribes.

Even as the question of expansion was being discussed, it was observed that some sections within these categories, especially among Dalit communities, were not availing of the benefit of reservations; thus, some of the most disadvantaged caste groups in different regions were lagging behind, while others became beneficiaries of the reservation policy and were able to make greater progress. The decision to create sub-divisions within SC reservation was initially implemented in the state of Punjab. An order issued by the government of Punjab on 5 May 1975 read, '...Government have decided that henceforth, 50 per cent vacancies of the quota reserved for Scheduled Castes should be offered to Balmikis and Mazhibi Sikhs, if available, as a first preference from amongst the Scheduled Castes candidates'.[1]

Similarly, the government of Haryana issued an order in 1994:

> For the purpose of reservation in services, the Scheduled Castes in Haryana will be put in two categories i.e. Block 'A' and Block 'B'. Block 'B' will consist of Chamars, Jatia Chamars, Rahgars, Ramdasias, Ravidisias. Block 'A' will consist of remaining 36 Scheduled Castes.... Within the quota reserved for Scheduled Castes in direct recruitment to Govt. jobs 50% will be offered to candidates from Block 'A'. In case suitable candidates from Block 'A' are not available, candidates from Block 'B' may be recruited

> against these vacancies. Similarly, candidates from Block 'B' will be given preference in respect of the remaining 50% vacancies in case suitable candidates from Block 'B' are not available. Candidates from Block 'A' may be recruited against these vacancies.[2]

Another case where demands were raised for sub-categorisation of SCs pertains to undivided Andhra Pradesh. The state government issued a notice on 31 May 2000—Notification of Government of Andhra Pradesh: Rationalisation (Sub-Category) Act of Reservations Rules. Unlike Punjab and Haryana where only two sub-groups were created, the Andhra Pradesh government divided the Schedule into four groups. These policies had two implications for reservation to the Scheduled Castes: (i) a hierarchy of preferences was introduced, and (ii) if the seats were filled up by the preferred group, others within the Scheduled Caste ambit would be unable to avail of reservations.

However, four years after the implementation of these rules in Andhra Pradesh, the Supreme Court struck down all instances of sub-categorisation of the Scheduled Caste list on the grounds that the process was unconstitutional (Malamahanadu Registered Society v. State of Andhra Pradesh & Others 2004 Civil Appeal 7344/2000).[3] Despite this, similar policies were enacted in the early 2000s. In 2007, the Bihar government termed 18 castes within the Schedule as 'Mahadalit'. In 2008, the Tamil Nadu government in principle accepted the report of the Justice M. S. Janardhanam Commission that recommended providing reservation for Arundathiyars within the existing SC quota (Viswanathan 2009).

It must be pointed out that every policy has its own politics through which it is brought into the public domain. Rao, for instance, therefore argues that 'the fanatic and haste… with which states have acted (some extremely successfully, others abortive, while still other evolved novel models) points to the new dangerous trend in caste politics' (2009: 37). However, what comes to the fore is that the division of castes and emergence of new castes and caste formations are bound to impact any policy's initiation and implementation. This will in turn have its implications on the emerging sociopolitical scenario. The operation of policy in a highly stratified society like India will invariably be rife with contradictions, and while these contradictions may not be permanent, they tend to get produced (and reproduced) by underlying sociopolitical circumstances. Thus, addressing these finer points purely objectively may be difficult, if not impossible.

Vertical Expansion

The expansion of reservation has not merely been horizontal—benefiting those standing on the same footing, but not included in the policy paradigm in the beginning—but also vertical, wherein the policy brought into its ambit other groups considered 'low' in the caste hierarchy. What needs to be recognised is that Indian society is characterised by multiple forms of exclusion, associated with group identities like caste, ethnicity, gender, religion, etc., in various spheres. This has implications for our society, polity, and economy. Therefore, a policy was required to address and overcome deprivation associated with these forms of exclusion. Development in post-independence India has benefited various groups in a differentiated manner. With the passage of time, those who experienced exclusion or derived limited benefits from social and economic development began seeking solutions to their group-specific problems.

Policy formation for various caste groups needs to take into account special features of the caste system and its exclusionary character that have had far-reaching social and economic consequences. The core governing principle of caste system is not inequality alone, but rather, 'graded inequality', that is, a system of hierarchical, unequal entitlement of rights to various caste groups.[4] Rights were not universal in this stratified social order. The system of graded entitlement to rights resulted in differentiation in the social, economic, and educational conditions of different castes (Thorat and Kumar 2008:17–18).

How should one develop inclusive and effective policies for different groups suffering from exclusion associated with caste, ethnicity, religion, and gender? This has been a key issue for policy-makers in India.

Within Hindu society, the principle of 'graded inequality' implies that not all castes suffer to the same degree from hierarchal entitlement of rights. The groups located at the bottom of caste hierarchy, namely the Dalits, have suffered the worst of caste prohibitions including the practice of untouchability. The Shudras, who primarily fall in the OBC category, follow closely; however, the discrimination faced by them differed in character and magnitude. While they were not the targets of practices like untouchability and residential and social isolation, historically they too faced exclusion in education, employment, and other spheres. Although the caste system is intrinsically connected to Hinduism, caste discrimination has carried over across religious boundaries in the Indian subcontinent and therefore persists among Christian and Muslim communities. However, the ways in which caste discrimination manifests are different.

Variations in the forms and spheres of discrimination have different consequences on the deprivation and poverty across various historically oppressed groups. There are few and limited studies on discrimination faced by non-SC/ST backward groups. Nevertheless, the unevenness of human development indicators across groups reflects patterns of historical discrimination in terms of differential access to income and income earning assets, property, business, employment, education, etc. Consequently, all such groups require corrective measures that can counter the historical denial of rights and also provide necessary safeguards against present-day discrimination. Thus, the reservation policy varies depending on the nature of discrimination faced by each of these excluded groups and their social, educational, economic, and political standing. Further, it is important to note that certain other categories like semi-nomadic communities and denotified tribes have faced serious forms of exclusion as well and require an inclusive policy. The following discussion describes inclusive policy recommendations and varying degrees of implementation.

Kaka Kalelkar Commission Report

To understand the Kaka Kalelkar Commission, we need to know the reasons for its formation and its larger context. One reason was probably the resignation of Ambedkar from Prime Minister Jawaharlal Nehru's Union Cabinet in 1951; Ambedkar stated that one of the reasons for his resignation was that the government was ignoring the interests of the backward classes. He made a statement on the floor of the House:

> I will now refer to another matter that had made me dissatisfied with the Government. It relates to the treatment accorded to the Backward Classes and the Scheduled Castes. I was very sorry that the Constitution did not embody any safeguards for the Backward Classes. It was left to be done by the Executive Government on the basis of the recommendations of a Commission to be appointed by the President. More than a year has elapsed since we passed the Constitution. But the Government has not even thought of appointing the Commission. (Ambedkar 1995, vol. 14: 1319)

Three years after the adoption of the Constitution, with provisions to identify the members of socially and educationally backward classes, the first policy decision in this direction was taken with the formation of the First Backward Classes Commission. The commission was set up by a presidential order on 29 January 1953, and is commonly known by the name of its chairperson, Kaka Kalelkar. Its objectives were

1. to determine the criteria to identify socially and educationally backward classes or communities or groups apart from SCs and STs;
2. to investigate their conditions to propose recommendations for removing barriers to their progress; and
3. to present a report to the President for implementation of measures for the inclusion of poor people of different classes.

The commission's mandate shows that its recommendations were meant for marginalised groups other than those already included in the constitutional Schedules. Accordingly, the commission used the following methods or the criteria to identify such classes:

1. Low social status based on caste hierarchy
2. Low level of education in the community
3. Inadequate representation in government jobs
4. Inadequate representation in businesses

Affirmative action policies initiated in colonial India already recognised the problems of low social status in the caste hierarchy and consequent low level of education and inadequate representation in government jobs. However, the commission added another major dimension of measuring exclusion: inadequate representation in businesses. This was a major departure from earlier criteria on the identification of backward classes in India.

The commission submitted its report on 30 March 1955. It had prepared a list of 2,399 'backward castes', of which 837 were classified as 'most backward'. In the absence of new data, the caste-wise distribution of population was based on the census of 1931. The social status of communities in the caste hierarchy was the basis of selection of beneficiaries' castes. The commission considered all women to be a part of the backward classes. In its report, the Kalelkar Commission recommended 70 per cent reservation in technical and professional institutions. Besides, there were to be reservations in all government employment and local bodies, in which 25 per cent, 33.5 per cent and 40 per cent seats were to be reserved for various groups clubbed under Classes I, II, III, and IV. It further recommended extensive government policies or programmes for the well-being and welfare of people, aimed at adult education, provision of rural housing, improved public healthcare, support for managing agriculture and livestock, etc.

Apart from these recommendations, the Kalelkar Commission made some significant observations. It argued that there should be a uniform policy across India to usher in social transformations that would account for backward classes. Presenting a list of backward and extremely backward classes, the report emphasised that these groups did not possess land, money, or industrial means. Rather than having 'protectors' from dominant classes, these groups required self-representation. The commission suggested that the privileged classes must voluntarily surrender their privilege, and that production and distribution networks should be on a socialist basis. It asserted that a secular democracy was necessarily based on mutual respect, trust, and service, and that leaders were needed from every community to ensure social justice and bring about a sense of 'universal brotherhood'.[5]

The government rejected these recommendations on the grounds that they were solely based on caste. The dominant view of the time was that the individual, or perhaps the family—rather than caste—should be seen as the 'unit' of backwardness. Jawaharlal Nehru, a modernist, was of the opinion that emphasis on 'primitive' identities like caste to measure backwardness would only strengthen caste distinctions. It was assumed that other sections of society who are financially weak would be deprived of coming under the purview of reservation benefits. In 1961, the union government decided against drawing any list of backward classes. States were advised to draw up their own lists of backward classes on the basis of economic condition rather than caste.

Demands by the lower and middle classes began to gather momentum for the demand of reservations for socially and economically backward classes in the 1980s, with Kanshi Ram and the All India Backward and Minority Communities Employees Federation (BAMCEF) playing a key role. Although they found some success with reservations being implemented at the state level, they continued to raise their demands until the implementation of the Mandal Commission recommendations in 1990 at the national level.

Mandal Commission Report

The 1977 general election was historic as for the first time a non-Congress political coalition formed government at the Centre. This was the Janata Party, a broad conglomeration of various political parties. The Second Backward Classes Commission was set up on 1 January 1979 by this government, during the term of

Prime Minister Morarji Desai. Bindeshwari Prasad Mandal headed the Commission and so it came to be known as the Mandal Commission. Out of the five members of the Commission, four belonged to backward classes, and one was a Dalit leader. The main objective of the Mandal Commission was to identify socially and educationally backward classes and to suggest measures to rectify their deprivation through reservations.

The commission adopted 11 criteria, grouped under three major categories:

Social Criteria

This included castes/classes

1. that were considered socially backward by others;
2. which mainly depended on manual labour for their livelihood;
3. where underage marriages were far higher than the state average; and
4. among whom the female work participation rate was at least 25 per cent greater than the state average.

Educational Criteria

Under this category, the commission identified castes/classes

1. where the number of children in the age group of 5–15 years who never attended school was at least 25 per cent higher than the state average;
2. with a student drop-out rate in the age group of 5–15 years that was at least 25 per cent above the state average; and
3. among whom the proportion of matriculates was at least 25 per cent lower than the state average.

Economic Criteria

The commission focused on castes/classes

1. where the average value of family assets was at least 25 per cent lower than the state average;
2. where the proportion of families living in *kuccha* houses is at least 25 per cent above the state average.
3. where 50 per cent of households live over half a kilometre away from a source of potable water.
4. where the number of households having taken consumption loans is at least 25 per cent above the state average.

The commission found that the imbalance between socially and economically advanced families and backward families was being reproduced across generations. Over a period of time, children coming from privileged backgrounds would have a distinct advantage in open competition in terms of 'merit' because they received enough resources to enhance their knowledge.

The commission submitted its report in December 1980. Among its main observations and recommendations were:

1. The estimated population of OBCs in India was 52 per cent including both Hindus and non-Hindus;
2. To remain within the 50 per cent ceiling on reservations, 27 per cent seats should be reserved for OBCs;
3. A total of 3,743 communities were included in the category;
4. Candidates recruited on the basis of open merit, even if hailing from communities that are beneficiaries of reservation, should not fall under reservation;
5. The aforesaid reservation should be made extended to all levels of promotion quotas;

6. Reserved positions that remain unfulfilled can be forward for three years and then de-reserved. The age limit for direct recruitment should be raised;
7. The roster system should be adopted for each category of posts;
8. Reservation is applied for public sector recruitment, educational institutions, and government-aided private institutions;
9. Adult education should be promoted through an intensive programme; and
10. Residential schools should be set up with all facilities free of cost; vocational training should be provided.

To address structural problems related to caste, the commission recommended some general measures as well. This included providing suitable finance and technical assistance at the institutional level to those wishing to set up small-scale industry. Separate financial institutions were recommended to provide special training to OBC candidates. The radical transformation of existing relations of production was considered the single most important step for the welfare and upliftment of all backward classes. Further, the Mandal Commission urged state governments to enact progressive laws (Ramaiah 2008: 154–156). Significantly, on the question of redistribution of land, it argued that surplus land should be distributed not only to Dalit and tribal landless labourers, but also to those from the Other Backward Classes. The commission also recommended that the central government should finance programmes for the betterment of OBC groups on the lines of existing programmes for SC and ST groups. These were important recommendations that went beyond the scope of existing policy, but they were seen as helpful in realising the full potential of reservations (ibid.).

In 1980, when Janata Party lost the parliamentary elections and the Congress formed government once again, the matter of reservation for OBCs was set aside and the Mandal Commission recommendations were not implemented. This was despite a statement by its chairperson that 'in case the report of my commission also meets the same fate as that of Kaka Kalelkar's Commission the legitimate hopes and aspirations of the socially and educationally backward classes, which constitute a bulk of the population will be dashed to ground' (Report of the First Backward Classes Commission 1980: 4). Even after the submission of the report, B. P. Mandal found a major lacuna between the promises of the government and implementation of the commission's basic recommendations. He stated: 'I was informed that it had been decided that caste enumeration will not be carried out during the 1981 census and the present policy of not having enumeration of caste in Indian Census will be continued, needs reconsideration' (ibid.). The government of the day was not serious about the implementation of the report.

In 1990, Prime Minister V. P. Singh initiated policy changes and announced reservations for OBCs. The implementation of Mandal Commission recommendations was a milestone for the socially and economically backward communities as it paved the way for the government to make new laws and policies specifically for their benefit.

Supreme Court Verdict on Mandal Commission

The implementation of the Mandal Commission recommendations was challenged in the Supreme Court by a writ petition. The case, officially known as Indra Sawhney v. Union of India & Others (1992), set an important precedent as it reiterated the legal validity of the recommendations. A major issue before the court was to adjudicate whether caste in itself can be considered as a determinant of a class. The challenge also sought to determine whether Article 16(4), which provides for affirmative action for backward classes, is in violation of Article 16 (1) which guarantees equality of opportunity in matters of public employment.

The petition argued that any policy of reservation on the basis of caste will only strengthen caste consciousness. They also put forward a common argument that the continuation of a reservation policy would sideline the question of merit and lead to a fall in standards. The government in its defence argued that implementing the report grants an opportunity to backward classes to fulfil their just claims to equal representation and participation. It also cited the First Backward Classes Report (1955), which had also recommended affirmative action as a means to undo the historical wrongs that backward classes have faced.

Limiting the Quota

Yet another important aspect of reservation has been the limit on quotas in terms of percentage. In a landmark verdict (Balaji v. State of Mysore [1962]), the Supreme Court interpreted the quota as a measure to promote the interests of all of society by promoting the interests of its most disadvantaged elements. It suggested that reservations should not exceed more than 50 per cent. In another important case, Devadasan v. Union of India (1964), the court stated that a quota that exceeded 50 per cent would be 'unconstitutional'. This position was also reiterated in Indra Sawhney v. Union of India verdict. Another important development soon after the implementation of OBC reservations came in 1991, when the Congress-ruled government issued a notification allocating 10 per cent reservation to 'economically deprived sections of the population' who were not covered by any existing affirmative action policy. However, in the case of Indra Sawnhey v. Union of India (1992), the Supreme Court struck down this provision, holding that economic factors cannot be the sole criterion for backwardness and must be evaluated along with or in addition to social backwardness. In its judgement, the Supreme Court stated:

> Just as every power must be exercised reasonably and fairly, the power conferred by Clause (4) of Article 16 should also be exercised in a fair manner and within reasonably limits—and what is more reasonable than to say that reservation under Clause (4) shall not exceed 50% of the appointments or posts, barring certain extra-ordinary situations as explained hereinafter.... The provision under Article 16(4)—conceived in the interest of certain sections of society—should be balanced against the guarantee of equality enshrined in Clause (1) of Article 16 which is a guarantee held out to every citizen and to the entire society. It is relevant to point out that Dr. Ambedkar himself contemplated reservation being 'confined to a minority of seats' (See his speech in Constituent Assembly, set out in para 28). No other member of the Constituent Assembly suggested otherwise. It is, thus clear that reservation of a majority of seats was never envisaged by the founding fathers. Nor are we satisfied that the present context requires us to depart from that concept.

The Court maintained that while the ceiling on reservations should be 50 per cent, there may be exceptional circumstances arising from the diversity of India and its people that necessitate a modification of the rule. However, extra caution must be used and a unique case must be established. Thus, reservation could exceed this upper limit only after the special consideration of the parliament, for example in the case of Tamil Nadu. However, in 2019 when a 10 per cent quota was created for the EWS category through a Parliamentary Act, the Court held that the legislation was legally valid and few questioned its validity. Thus, reservations in education and public employment now stand at 60 per cent.

Creamy Layer as a Policy and Sub-Categorisation among OBCs

The most significant group for whom expansion of the policy has been crucial and controversial remain the Other Backward Classes. Defining this category has proved to be a persistent challenge from the beginning. From the 1920s to 1950s, there was little demand to make provisions for this class due to the heterogeneity of social and financial status within the group. Much later, after the implementation of OBC reservations, there were contestations within this category, especially regarding the idea that the 'well-off' among the category were eligible for reservations.

Although the Constitution of India mandated the inclusion of backward groups in the ambit of policy, as discussed earlier, it was necessary to find out the status of the community and required measures. The backward classes remain an extremely fluid category. Thus, there are a few important considerations when analysing OBC reservations. *First*, there is no specific data on the caste-based composition of the population, barring a few older sources such as the 1931 national census. *Second*, as discussed earlier, although OBC groups were socially and educationally backward, they did not suffer from practices like untouchability and physical segregation. *Third*, political reservations were not a major demand of OBCs, who instead focused on issues of employment and education. *Fourth*, reservation policy has been focused on communities facing various forms of social discrimination rather than economic status. Even as the Mandal Commission Report expanded the ambit of reservations for a number of backward class communities, the court introduced the concept of 'creamy layer' which effectively restricted its application. This was a sub-classification based on economic status. The 'creamy layer' category comprises OBCs who are economically advanced and whose annual income exceeds a fixed upper limit. People falling in this sub-category are excluded from availing the benefits of OBC reservation. The Sattanathan Commission first used the term 'creamy layer' in 1971, stating that people belonging to this social stratum are not to be included in the list of beneficiaries (Gupta 2012). The Justice Ram Nandan Committee reiterated this view in 1993 (ibid.). The Supreme Court defined the creamy layer, quoting an Indian governmental office memorandum dated 8 September 1993. The term was first legally deployed in the context of reservation of jobs for certain groups in Indra Sawhney and Others v. Union of India case in 1992. According to the Supreme Court, it applied to children of constitutional functionaries, such as the President, judges of the Supreme Court and High Courts, employees of central and state bureaucracies above a certain grade, public sector employees, and members of the armed forces and paramilitary personnel above the rank of colonel. The creamy layer would be updated by reviewing the gross annual income of parents. If the gross annual income of parents fell below a pre-defined ceiling for three consecutive years, the children would be able to avail of reservation.

The National Commission for Backward Classes (NCBC) proposed two recommendations in October 2015 with respect to OBCs. *First*, it recommended that the upper limit on gross annual income of parents should be Rs 15,00,000. *Second*, OBCs should be sub-categorised into three groups—backward, more backward, and extremely backward—with an appropriate quota allotted to each sub-group (NCBC Report 2015).

The Ministry of Social Justice and Empowerment examines the income ceiling in every three years. In March 2019, a panel was appointed by the Ministry, headed by retired secretary B. P. Sharma, to review the gross annual income limit and 'revisit the criteria' used to identify the creamy layer. In order to enable participation of the poorest of the poor in reserved categories, the panel considered revising the salary and income criteria. At present, as per its recommendations in 2020, the income ceiling has been lowered to Rs 8,00,000.

In 2006, the central government introduced reservations for OBCs in educational institutions. A public interest litigation (PIL) was filed in the Supreme Court challenging reservations in professional educational institutions. On 29 March 2007, the Court ordered an interim stay on the provision until the verdict was announced. On 10 April 2008, the Supreme Court ruled that the quotas introduced by the government are constitutionally valid and will apply to government institutions such as the Indian Institutes of Technology (IITs) and Indian Institutes of Management (IIMs), excluding the creamy layer in the case of OBCs.

Changing Nomenclature of Claimants

From its inception to the present day, different terms have been used to define the beneficiaries of reservation policy. This has ranged from non-Brahmins and Depressed Classes in the pre-independence period to Scheduled Castes, Scheduled Tribes, Other Backward Classes, and Economically Weaker Sections.

Backward Classes

Defining Backward Classes was a complex problem. Initially, the category was seen to include all non-Brahmins, with caste being the main determinant. During the Constituent Assembly debates the issue was debated and a provision was made under Article 340 that says, 'The President may by order appoint a Commission consisting of such persons as he thinks fit to investigate the conditions of socially and educationally backward classes within the territory of India....' This was in addition to the Scheduled Castes and Scheduled Tribes, who had been specifically mentioned under different provisions of the Constitution. The first Constitutional Amendment under Article 15(4) introduced mechanisms to legislate any special provisions for the Backward Classes, SCs and STs. It was in response to an adverse judgment against the provisions of reservations by the Supreme Court in the State of Madras v. Shrimati Champakam Dorairajan (1951) and Venkataraman v. the State of Madras (1969) cases. This gave a broader outlook to the category of Backward Classes.

Scheduled Tribes

The Scheduled Tribes is a broad grouping that designates those who are thought to be the 'original inhabitants' of the land. Many tribal communities use the term 'Adivasi'. The Schedule protects communities who, in terms of social, cultural, religious, and linguistic practices, are distinct from the 'mainstream' of society and have historically been isolated from it. Initially, according to the Government of India Act, 1935, tribes were part of the Scheduled Castes. However, in the Constitution of independent India, the list was reclassified and a separate category of Scheduled Tribes was created.

Another important component relates to Scheduled Areas and categorising the inhabitants of the area as belonging to the Scheduled Tribes. Prior to independence, the Government of India Act, 1935 termed them 'Excluded Areas' or 'Partially Excluded

Areas' to protect them from exploitation by outsiders (Galanter 1984: 147). The Fifth and Sixth Schedules of the Constitution of India define the process of categorising any area as a Scheduled Area. The President of India can add and also de-schedule areas. The objective is to retain the distinct ways of life associated with different tribes and protect their cultural heritage.

Other Backward Classes

Other Backward Classes (OBCs) remains a fluid category. However, the OBCs are categorised on the basis of two factors: *first*, due to their status as a group of communities who require special provisions for socioeconomic improvement, and *second*, as castes who are discriminated against for 'low' status, although they are still seen as part of varna society. During the Constituent Assembly debates over the inclusion of 'backward' classes, state governments were given the authority to decide on whether particular communities come under the purview of reservation or not. Some states had conferred benefits and expanded reservations to backward classes even before the Constitution came into effect. These states include Bihar and Uttar Pradesh, which provided reservations in 1947 and 1948 respectively.

By the 1970s, at least 13 states provided reservations to the OBCs (Galanter 1984: 87). Various state governments set up Backward Classes Commissions that worked on the basis of economic criteria. Ram Manohar Lohia, a socialist leader, demanded 60 per cent reservation for the backward classes. He gave the slogan '*Sansopa ne bandhi gaath, pichhda pave sau mein saath*' (Sansopa [the Samyukta Socialist Party] is determined, the backward should get 60 out of 100). As we have discussed earlier, in 1978, the Mandal Commission was set up to examine the question of an OBC quota at the national level and in 1990, an OBC quota was implemented based on its recommendations. Consequently, the National Commission for Backward Classes Act (Act No. 27 of 1993) was enacted by the government to set up a permanent National Commission for Backward Classes (NCBC).

Referring to the multidimensional contours of the term, Deshpande points out that the Mandal Commission Report, the National Commission for Backward Classes, and the Supreme Court suggest a set of 'neutral' criteria namely poverty, place of habitation, occupation, and income level, which need to be used to determine backwardness, rather than just caste but it remains the core definition (Deshpande 2013: 127). Now OBC may be understood in terms of Backward Classes based on both caste and religion, other than SC/ST who are not part of the creamy layer and the threshold of it is decided from time to time.

Most Backward Classes

The concept of Most Backward Classes (MBC) was driven by the fact that 'Backward Classes' as a category is not being uniform. There was a need to distinguish between the relatively better-placed and worse-off. The first such division was recommended by the Kaka Kalelkar Commission, who created a sub-category called Most Backward Castes; as a policy this was implemented in Tamil Nadu. The dominance of non-Brahmin upper castes in the state apparatus pushed the Dravida Munnetra Kazhagam (DMK)-ruled state government to appoint the A. N. Sattanathan Commission in 1969. The commission observed that

> nearly 70 per cent of the population of the cultivating castes, i.e., Padayachi, Kallar and Maravar and a large percentage of the Valiyans, Ambalakarans and Boyas; more than half the Kaikola population; and the numerous smaller castes, including barbers and washermen, living in conditions of abject squalor and under

conditions hardly distinguishable from those prevailing amongst the Scheduled Castes before Independence. (Government of Tamil Nadu 1971: 50–51)

However, policies based on this observation were not implemented for 20 years after the report was submitted. After winning the 1989 Assembly election and once again forming government, the DMK-ruled state government appointed another commission that recommended a division of reserved seats between Backward and Most Backward Classes (Government of Tamil Nadu 1985: 378–379). Accordingly, the state government ordered that out of the total OBC reservation, 20 per cent should be set aside for 39 communities listed as MBCs.

Demands for the Extension of OBC Reservations

Several communities, notably the Patidars of Gujarat, the Jats of Haryana, and the Marathas of Maharashtra have in the last few years been agitating for inclusion under the OBC category. In 2015, when Jats demanded reservations in the central government jobs and educational institutions, the Supreme Court rejected their demands, stating that they were not socially and economically deprived in comparative terms and pointed out that they were already included in the OBC category in nine states. The Supreme Court also rejected a review plea by the government that challenged this verdict (Ram Singh v. Union of India 2015). This verdict triggered a widespread agitation with occasional eruptions of violence. The Haryana state government approved a statute in 2016 that provided reservation to Jats and five other groups by classifying them as 'backward classes'. However, the High Court of Punjab and Haryana blocked the legislation, stating that reservations would then exceed the Supreme Court's 50 per cent ceiling (Rajan 2019). In November 2018, the Maharashtra state assembly passed a measure granting the Marathas 16 per cent quota in higher education and public sectors, with an overwhelming majority of MLAs in favour of the provision (*Business Standard* 2018; Rajan 2019). However, a similar quota created for the community in 2014 was struck down by the Bombay High Court citing the 50 per cent ceiling (Rajan 2019).

In 2015, another dominant caste group, the Patels in Gujarat, launched a protest to demand quotas in public employment. In the early stages of the protest, a gathering of over 25,000 individuals from the Patel community mobilised in support of this demand. The first major event in this protest was a demonstration in Visnagar, which became controversial due to the associated violence (*Business Standard* 2018). In 2016, a year later, other dominant castes in different parts of India also began to raise demands for reservation. Their protests were non-violent; rallies were organised at the district level. More than 1.2 million people were mobilised in total (Jaffrelot and A. K. 2017). The Kapus of Andhra Pradesh, for instance, demanded affirmative action in public sector jobs.

Interestingly, the BJP, whose parent organisation, the Rashtriya Swayamsevak Sangh (RSS) has consistently argued that caste-based reservations would divide society (*The Hindu* 2015), has sought to implement class-based reservations in states where the party is in power. In 2015, the Rajasthan Economically Backward Classes (Reservation of Seats in Educational Institutions in the State and of Appointments and Posts in Services under the State) Bill was passed (ibid.). Similarly, the governments of Gujarat and Maharashtra, where BJP has been in power either independently or in coalition, also proposed reservations for economically disadvantaged groups. However, the courts overruled these proposals (*The Wire* 2018; *Times of India* 2018).

Strangely, in March 2021, B. Sriramulu, Social Welfare Minister of the Karnataka government where BJP was in power, stated that 'the demand by some groups to provide reservation to various communities in proportion to their population is justified'. Similar to the Gurjar demand to be included in the ST list in Rajasthan, in the context of Karnataka, Sriramulu stated:

> Several communities are asking for higher quantum of reservation or re-categorisation of reservation. Kurubas are demanding to be listed under Scheduled Tribes, while Panchamsali Lingayats are demanding to be moved to 2A from 3B among Backward Classes. Leaders of these communities are saying that such issues could be resolved if the total quantum of reservation increased. There are suggestions that SC reservation be increased to 17%, ST to 7.5%, and the total reservation slab could be increased in proportion of other backward castes. The State government is considering all these suggestions.... (*The Hindu* 2021)

Senior Cabinet members such as Jagadish Shettar have advocated for the inclusion of Kurubas on the Scheduled Tribes list. Following a long struggle, the Rajasthan state government granted Gurjars and four other nomadic communities—Banjara, Gadia-Lohar, Raika, and Gadariya—a 5 per cent quota in jobs and education by establishing a 'Most Backward Class' category for them (*Economic Times* 2022). Thus, the implementation of reservations is rife with complexity and requires specific policy solutions in the Indian context.

Reservations for Women in Local Bodies

Reservations for women were introduced in local government bodies, both in rural and urban areas, through the 73rd and 74th Constitutional Amendments in 1992. This step brought a necessary gender perspective to reservation policy. There have been contestations and debates about the efficacy of such representation, especially in patriarchal contexts across India where women are seen as 'dependent' on their husbands or male relatives when taking decisions. However, one needs to understand that over a period of time, and with greater access to education and public participation, women occupying reserved positions in local bodies have become more assertive.

Women's reservations in the Parliament and state assemblies was a matter of extended debate for over two decades. The passage of the Constitution (106th Amendment) Act by the Parliament in September 2023 was a crucial boost to the reservation policy. The Act has instituted women's reservations in both national and state legislative bodies, although this will only come into effect after the delimitation exercise to be carried out in 2026. Those who do not support such reservations again contend that 'separate constituencies for women would not only narrow their outlook but lead to perpetuation of unequal status because they would be seen as not competing on merit' (PRS Legislative Research 2023). Women's reservations may gradually be normalised, like the political reservations for SC/STs. However, the question of intersectionality still remains unresolved as women from OBC and minority groups do not get exclusive reservation—only SC/ST women will be eligible for reservation from among the existing political reservations for their communities in the Lok Sabha and state assemblies. Thus, the general acceptance of the reservation policy as a norm is established, in spite of occasional controversy.

Reservation for Economically Weaker Section (EWS)

As discussed earlier, the Congress in 1991 sought to grant reservations purely on an economic basis, but the Supreme Court ruled that its decision was unconstitutional. In 2019, just months before the Lok Sabha elections, the NDA-I government moved a Bill to grant 10 per cent reservation to EWS candidates (within the unreserved or 'general' category) in government positions and educational institutions. The legislation was in addition to the pre-existing 50 per cent quota for SC/ST/OBC categories. The 124th Amendment Bill, 2019, was introduced in the Lok Sabha on 8 January 2019; the process in both Houses of Parliament and the President's assent were carried out in a record four days. The EWS reservation marks a significant turning point, since it is a class-based category, whereas the major categories previously created were based on caste. A number of state governments rapidly approved the legislation and others stated their desire to implement it.

Various conditions have been laid down to ensure that EWS reservation is precisely defined within the larger policy framework, as detailed in Rajan (2019):

1. the yearly household income of the candidate must be less than Rs 8,00,000;
2. the beneficiary's family should not possess more than 5 acres of farmland;
3. the area of any residential flat in their ownership should be less than 1,000 square feet;
4. in case the residential plot is in a notified municipality sector, the area shall be less than 100 square yards; for a non-notified municipality sector, the area should be less than 200 square yards.

Reservations in the Private Sector

Reservations in private institutions were introduced through the 93rd Constitutional Amendment, which came into effect in 2006.

The amendment inserted a clause in Article 15 of the Constitution specifying that special provisions can be made

> for the advancement of socially and educationally backward classes of citizens or for the Scheduled Castes or the Scheduled Tribes in so far as such special provisions relate to their admission to educational institutions including private educational institutions, whether aided or unaided by the State [except in minority institutions].

Despite there being a provision in the Constitution, the central government has not taken any legislative action to implement this in letter or spirit. In 2019, the government asserted that reservations for SCs, STs, OBCs, and EWS categories will be extended to private colleges in the future (Rajan 2019).

Summing Up

There has been both extension and expansion of reservation policy in India. As mentioned earlier, an important aspect of public perception is the shift in certain groups from vehement opposition to acceptance and even demands to be included within the reservations framework. This is true in the case of both dominant and 'upper' castes, who were at the forefront of anti-reservation protests in 1990, but now seek categorisation under the OBC or EWS categories. Another puzzle is the demand of OBCs for inclusion in the ST list both in Rajasthan and Karnataka. These details are discussed in the next chapter.

Notes

1. Notification of Government of Punjab Regarding Sub-Classification Letter No. 1818-SWI-75/10451, dated 5 May 1975.

2. Letter no. 22/55/90-3GS-III, dated 9 November 1994, from the Chief Secretary, Government of Haryana to All Heads of Departments, Commissioners of Ambala, Hissar, Rohtak and Gurgaon Divisions and all Deputy Commissioners and Sub-Divisional Officers (Civil) in Haryana.

3. Malamahanadu Registered Society v. State of Andhra Pradesh & Others 2004 Civil Appeal 7344/2000.

4. This term was used by Ambedkar to explain the hierarchical entitlement of rights and duties in the caste system. The castes located at the bottom of the hierarchy, that is, Dalits, suffered the most, closely followed by various OBC groups. 'The caste system is marked not merely by inequality but is affected by the system of graded inequality. All castes are not on a par. They are one above the other. There is a kind of ascending scale of hatred and a descending scale of contempt' (Ambedkar 1979, vol. 1: 167).

5. The full report is available at https://dspace.gipe.ac.in/xmlui/handle/10973/33678 (accessed May 2024).

three

Challenges of Implementation

The policy of reservations was adopted in the Indian Constitution as a measure to address prevailing inequalities. Yet, as noted in the Introduction, the irony is that even seven decades after its implementation, the dominant discussion on reservations still revolves around its legitimacy, and hence remains stuck on questions about its relevance, essence, and guiding principles. How this policy paradigm has contributed to the development of marginalised sections in India is a question that remains largely unexplored.[1] In other words, the overarching focus has been on the very idea of reservations and hence administrative aspects related to the policy are generally ignored. This chapter shows how the administrative aspect of reservation policy is closely intertwined with its principles. In discussing this policy, it is imperative to discuss its implementation at various levels.

The procedural aspects of reservation policy continue to be seen as purely a domain of bureaucratic process. This leaves room for interpretation and misinterpretation of the issue by the state governments, ministries, or institutions enacting the policy. Implementation in this sense may not be free of various biases or prejudices. This chapter shall highlight the few institutional mechanisms that have been devised for implementation. It remains to be seen how effective they have been. Despite constitutional obligations, reserved seats at various levels are often not filled up. At various levels of recruitment, especially in the state services, implementation of the reservation policy remains limited due to various reasons. Similarly, in educational institutions, OBC reservations were implemented as late as 2006. Even for SC and ST reservations, the University of Delhi implemented reservations in faculty recruitment at the level of Assistant Professors only in 1996, and the policy is yet to be implemented in the case of promotions. Despite bodies like the National Commission for Scheduled Castes, National Commission for Scheduled Tribes and National Commission for Other Backward Castes taking stock of the situation and calling attention to these issues in their reports, there was little headway. It was only in the late 1990s and early 2000s, when Dalit mobilisation emerged as a major political force, that the government at central and state levels began to take implementation seriously and action was taken.

This chapter argues that there are two-fold hindrances in the implementation of reservations. One set of hindrances is structural in nature and exists at the level of preconceived bias and prejudice. Such notional aspects have long-term repercussions, including psychological impact. These notional hindrances are explained here in terms of a two-fold marginalisation where the candidates who are covered by the reservation policy are disadvantaged in two ways. Instead of policy being a facilitator, it is converted into a mode of filtration and further exclusion. This double whammy has been defined here as the 'exclusion–discrimination duo'. Such micro-level hindrances operate within institutions. The second set of hindrances is institutional in character. Institutional hindrances are further divided into two: those that operate in national politics and the second at the micro institutional/organisational level.

The Exclusion–discrimination Duo

The biggest challenge to implementation emanates from two issues: exclusion and discrimination. The former is about non-representation of members of a group in certain public affairs, institutional affairs, or decision-making. Discrimination on the other hand is about a selective approach towards a group on the basis of its identity. Reservation as a policy intervention was expected to address both these problems, as discussed in Chapter 2. However, a closer look at the implementation of reservations shows that has not happened in practice. Merely implementing reservations in terms of achieving certain numbers may not be enough to make various spaces safe, accessible, and comfortable for marginalised groups. Instead, both these concerns require special attention and policy interventions. Non-implementation of reservation is not merely a game of numbers or about calculations. It is also about how this policy and its beneficiaries are perceived.

The initial challenge is to achieve representation of various sections of society across all levels of institutions and organisations. Not having a representative institution in itself poses a challenge to the legitimacy, efficiency, and effectiveness of any institution or organisation. Despite the fact that the reservation in services has been in place since independence, there are still public institutions, leave aside private ones, where there is little to no presence of people from different social groups. For example, in response to a recent question raised in Parliament, the Parliamentary Committee on Welfare of Scheduled Castes and Scheduled Tribes underlined that people from marginalised communities are absent from high-level positions in many prominent public sector undertakings (PSUs). While making this point, the report cited the board of directors of some of the biggest ventures of the Indian government, such as the State Bank of India and the Power Grid Corporation, where there is not even a single member belonging to the Scheduled Castes or Tribes (*The Indian Express* 2023).

In the case of marginalised groups, their individual capacity to perform well is not seen as a part of group behavior, unlike the 'upper' castes whose capacity is recognised as individual as well as traced to some 'collective capacity' to perform well. This also gets reflected in the fact that the ministries, departments and PSUs had to run special drives to fill up the reserved positions for the SC and ST. As highlighted in Tables 3.1 and 3.2, these drives were carried out continuously from the year 1991. In spite of this, the maximum rate of recruitment out of seats reserved for SCs was 50 per cent (and that too in promotions, as shown in Table 3.4). For autonomous bodies, the maximum rate was less than 30 per cent. The SC Commission has highlighted in its reports how autonomous bodies, especially PSUs, tend to avoid fulfilling their obligation to recruit candidates against reserved seats. In most of these cases, the positions are declared technical or research based (NCSC 2010: 173). In the existing legislation for reservations, there is an exemption for such positions. The commission highlighted that there is a need to check this trend.

Table 3.1: Representation of SCs and OBCs in Central Government Ministries/Departments (2015–2016)

Group	*Total employees*	*No of SC employees*	*Percentage of SC employees*	*No of OBC Employees*	*Percentage of OBC employees*
A	50,007	6,129	12.26	5,428	10.85
B	1,10,333	17,587	15.94	11,388	10.32
C (excluding *safai karamcharis*)	17,74,167	3,01,079	16.97	3,63,379	20.48
C (*safai karamcharis*)	42,340	17,366	41.02	5,472	12.92
Total	19,76,847	3,42,161	17.31	3,85,667	19.51

Source: NCSC Annual Report (2016: 211).

Table 3.2: Representation of STs in Central Government Ministries/Departments (as on 1 January 2015)

Group	*Total employees*	*No of ST employees*	*Percentage of ST employees*
A	72,378	4,211	5.82
B	2,18,558	14,667	6.72
C (excluding *safai karamcharis*)	28,38,999	2,44,368	8.61
C (*safai karamcharis*)	44,420	2,694	6.06
Total	31,74,335	2,65,960	8.38

Source: NCST Annual Report (2015: 254).

In addition, the question that does not get addressed in the majority of policy discourse is why there is a need to have special drives even five decades after reservation policy being put in place. Further, even when five special drives were conducted in one decade, quota seats remained vacant. In other words, in the decades after independence there was no political commitment to ensure representation of marginalised groups in various public institutions or public sector jobs. These special drives began only once the state had already expressed its intent to carry out neoliberal economic reforms and thereby move away from a state-centred economy in 1991. Thus, even as interest in fulfilling reservation obligations increased, at a broader level there was a gradual decline in public sector employment and the disinvestment process had already begun. Various reports of the National Commission for the Scheduled Castes show that employment in the government sector today is only about half of what existed in 1991–1992.

The NCSC in its 2016 report had shown the status of representation of various social sections in government jobs in different sectors. The data shows that despite legal and political battles, the number of employees from Scheduled Castes, Scheduled Tribes, Other Backward Classes remains low in all government sectors. The only segment where members

Table 3.3: Details of SC/ST Hiring in Special Recruitment Drive

Department	*Backlog vacancies identified*	*Appointment offers issued*	*Backlog (in %)*
Special recruitment drive no 1 (1989)			
Central govt	35,647	31,253	87
PSUs	11,000	8,125	73.90
Banks	8,822	8,084	91.60
Insurance companies	3,085	3,023	98
	58,554	50,485	86.22
Special recruitment drive no 2 (1990)			
Central govt	31,928	19,879	62.30
PSUs	10,461	6,316	60.40
Banks	3,142	2,197	69.90
Insurance companies	1028	1023	99.50
	46,559	29,415	63.18
Special recruitment drive no 3 (1991–92)			
Central govt	13,556	8,811	65
PSUs	12,149	7,195	57
Banks	2,242	1384	61.70
Insurance companies	804	381	47.40
	28,751	17,771	61.81

Source: National Commission for SC/ST Welfare Annual Report (2006: 79).

of the Scheduled Castes are adequately represented, or rather, overrepresented, are the group D posts, which primarily comprise peons and other supporting staff. The other category in which SCs are overrepresented is the jobs of cleaners or *safai karmcharis*.

A major reason cited for this imbalance is the alleged lack of candidates with the expertise or skills required for various positions. Due to persistent prejudice, candidates from marginalised sections are not considered worthy of the training and skill management required for technical and research-based jobs, leave aside hiring practices jobs of this nature. It is this prejudice that explains why autonomous bodies have not implemented reservations effectively. Policy discourse in India has not looked at the problem from the other side—the failure of marginalised sections to acquire training and skills does not throw their individual capacity into question, but reflects on the kind of institutional vision Indian institutions have had. Technical institutions have failed to develop effective and inclusive technical or pedagogical tools which can be user-friendly irrespective of students' background. In other words, instead of enabling empowerment, these bodies have become 'filtering institutions' that systematically exclude reserved candidates. Although this is beyond the scope of the present volume, further discussion is urgently required and we leave it as an open question.

To address both exclusion and discrimination, there should be special drives for recruitment, and along with this special training sessions and other policy supplements should be instituted for candidates from marginalised communities. However, prevailing social bias reflects the idea that members of certain privileged groups 'innately' possess greater skills by birth and influences recruitment patterns. Such assumptions hamper efforts for equal recognition and dignity.

The other issue associated with implementation is of notional change and awareness. The challenge of representation of various marginalised communities is just one side of the story. The students/candidates from marginalised communities face two-fold disadvantage. Such candidates have to face the challenge of caste discrimination which prevails outside the institution, and on the other hand they are met with prejudice within the institution for availing a quota that is associated with the caste. Thus, while pre-existing patterns of caste discrimination are there in any case, even after joining a particular institution, the stigma associated with quota-based recruitment also becomes attached to the candidate. This is not only about those whose performance is not the best. Even those who do perform well as per the metric set by institutions are stigmatised. A common refrain heard about well-performing marginalised students is that they are doing well 'despite being from SC/ST or backward castes' or 'despite being a woman'.[2]

In short, marginalised students and job-seekers are in the first place, victims of social discrimination in their social contexts. Second, they are discriminated against when they join institutions on a reserved position as people appointed through unreserved positions see them as 'undeserving'. They are also seen as people who have 'taken' the position of those who were otherwise 'deserving'.

In academic discourse nowadays, a distinction is made between caste-based discrimination and quota-based discrimination. It is argued in such cases that the challenges faced by marginalised students in educational institutions is not due to their caste but the anxiety and frustration among those who do not get benefit of quota.This logic is based on a very narrow and sectorally squeezed definition and understanding of discrimination based on caste. Such discussions about generalisations are usually based on surveys or studies of engineering or medical colleges (Bertrand et al. 2010; Sharma and Subramanyam 2020). They overlook the fact that where there is no such quota in admissions, oppressed caste students face extreme forms of discrimination. Among recently documented cases is one from Rajasthan where some schoolchildren were not allowed to drink water from the community source on the pretext that it was meant for children from 'upper castes' (*The Times of India* 2021). Such blatant practices of segregation are not limited to students. Teachers belonging to marginalised sections face similar kinds of exclusion,[3] even when people working in schools or others who are associated with the school are unaware of the quota from which a particular teacher has been appointed. The basis of discrimination is simply the caste of the teacher or student.

Having said that, the implementation of reservations creates its own complexities. These complexities are exacerbated by an insensitive institutional environment that still exists in India. Apart from the case of Scheduled Castes and Tribes, this can also be seen in case of institutional attitudes about persons with disability (PwD) and women. For those who fall in these categories, the discrimination is about their social responsibilities or physical status. Such candidates have to face comments questioning their innate skill and ability to work. Such interactions reflect prejudiced notions associated with various social groups, and caste remains among the most persistent sites of prejudiced thinking.

The discourse about problematising the quota system on the basis of anxiety and frustration of the privileged castes is quite misplaced as it tends to ignore the structural problems that lead to such outcomes. These psychological outcomes are produced by a masculinist, upper-caste/class identity formation premised on caste supremacy. The social milieu and cultural capital afforded to such a group creates an environment where they feel that access to any institution or the dream of upward socioeconomic mobility is their natural prerogative (*LiveLaw* 2021). Their social status brings along with it a preconceived bias of meritocracy whereby the privileged section considers itself meritorious and hence more deserving and 'civilised' as compared to other groups. In case such individuals are unable to get that they think belongs to them, blaming others who do not figure in this narrow social configuration is the only way to resolve their identity crisis and personal existential dilemma. It is not always about asserting one's caste identity in explicit terms. Such logic also includes being insensitive to variations in social background and access to social, cultural, and economic capital (or lack thereof) that is unequally distributed merely by virtue of birth.

This skewed perspective on structural problems culminates in privileged groups assuming a natural right to judge the stigmatised 'Others' who, according to them, do not deserve coveted institutional access. Demands for proportionate representation or better sensitised campuses in such scenario are not the point of discussion. Nor is the psychological health of those who are disempowered or need representation considered in this debate.

It is in this context that another significant challenge emerges in terms of implementation. Apart from the problem of ensuring representation of diverse social groups, there are no effective institutional mechanisms to challenge the understanding of those who come from socially dominant groups and are hence not eligible for reservations.There are no institutional mechanisms for sensitisation regarding various forms of social, cultural, or other forms of exclusion based on ascriptive identities.There are also no initiatives to create awareness amongst those who are eligible for these benefits. Currently, the policy of reservation is implemented through a bureaucratised process that makes availing of these entitlements a complicated, costly, tiring, and nontransparent process, and which leaves marginalised individuals vulnerable to harassment. Reports suggest that when faced with discrimination, many candidates decide not to follow up on any such cases of harassment or humiliation by their peers.

The two mechanisms set up to protect people covered by the reservation policy are (i) the concerned departmental/ institutional cell and (ii) the national commissions. Intra-institutional mechanisms are meant to be easy to access. However, in the absence of clear guidelines, protections, and procedures for their functioning, they remain mere tokens and are primarily bureaucratic bodies. This is one of the reasons that the intra-institutional disputes related to reservations such as drawing up of the roster, backlog in recruitment, etc., gets stuck in long-term litigation, resulting in delays in appointments. In most cases, it is the policy that gets blamed for such delays, not institutional hurdles; there is little conversation about improving the internal mechanisms meant for such purposes.

The Sectoral Divide

The reservation policy has been implemented at three major levels: central and state legislatures, local self-government bodies, and admissions in public-sector academic institutions and employment. Its implementation in the first two sectors has by and large been a success. In Parliament as well as state legislative assemblies, the question of reservation for marginalised groups (especially the Scheduled Castes and Tribes) has been in effect since independence. Similarly, in 1993 when the 73rd and 74th Constitutional Amendments were introduced for the local self-government bodies in cities and villages, provision for reservation has been implemented quite successfully.

Similarly, in the case of central services, the reservation policy is in effect. However, the representation of SCs and OBCs remains low. Those belonging to SC groups are highly represented (or overrepresented) in Category D jobs and under-represented in other categories. This phenomenon is prevalent across sectors of the economy and in various states of India.

Even in states with high Scheduled Caste populations like Punjab, Rajasthan, and Uttar Pradesh, representation of SCs in public employment is very poor. As Table 3.6 shows, for the majority of states with high SC population, there is a large gap in the number of seats for SC candidates versus the actual number of appointments.

Table 3.4: Number of Backlog Vacancies Identified and Filled (as in 2005)

Establishment	*Direct Recruitment*						*Promotion*					
	SC			*ST*			*SC*			*ST*		
	Identified	*Filled*	*% achieved*	*Identified*	*Filled*	*% achieved*	*Identified*	*Filled*	*% achieved*	*Identified*	*Filled*	*% achieved*
Ministries/ Departments including attached and subordinated offices	8510	4165	48.9	11312	4758	42	21130	10992	52	24795	6925	27.9
Autonomous bodies	4238	1124	26.5	4043	713	17.6	1053	277	26.3	1022	130	12.7
Total	12748	5289	41.4	15355	5291	34.4	22183	11269	50.8	25817	7055	27.3

Source: NCSC Annual Report (2006).

Table 3.5: Representation of SCs in State Government Enterprises (2015–2016)

States where representation is less than norms					
State name	*Norms*	*Group A*	*Group B*	*Group C*	*Group D*
Punjab	31.9	17.03	17.52	22.4	34.14
Himachal Pradesh	25.2	12.4	16.9	17.96	25.77
West Bengal	23	12.86	15.05	21	22.21
Uttar Pradesh	20.7	12.17	15.03	17.77	37.95
Tamil Nadu	20.01	7.4	13.43	15.79	29.87
Haryana	18.9	8.66	10.69	12.52	23.76
Rajasthan	17.16	7.64	8.24	8.26	17.21
Odisha	17.13	6.33	12.38	12.85	18.28
Chattisgarh	12.82	11.02	12.58	13.35	22.11
Representation near the norms					
Karnataka	17.15	18.17	15.31	15.72	24.41
Madhya Pradesh	15.62	12.31	16.19	15.91	24.03
Andhra Pradesh	15	14.83	0	15.87	28
Maharashtra	10.02	15.33	14.06	13.16	16.47
Bihar	7.09	8.24	8.26	17.21	80.91

Source: NCSC Annual Report (2016: 215).

In the case of South Indian states, the number of SC candidates in services is close to the government defined norms. For instance, in Karnataka the norm is 17.15 per cent and the actual number of SCs in services in all four grades is higher than this requirement. Maharashtra fares similarly. In the case of north India, Bihar is the only state where the representation of SCs in services is quite close to the stipulated quota. This may well be due to very low representation being the norm: In Bihar, it is set at 7.09 per cent. In states like Punjab where the norm is 31.9 per cent, the norms are quite high to begin with (NCSC Annual Report 2016: 214).

Do these trends have correlations with regional variations in social reform movement and political mobilisation of the Dalits that happened during the colonial period? The Ambedkarite movement and mobilisation led by Phule's Satyashodhak Samaj are two major examples that likely had some influence on the performance of reservation policy in Maharashtra. These are hypothetical answers that may form the crux of future research agendas.

Although there are instances of conflict regarding the reservation policy for promotions, the provision has been implemented in the all-India services. The major arena of confrontation for the last four decades has been the implementation of affirmative action policies in academic institutions. In both admission as well as recruitment, there have been roadblocks in implementation, attempts to scuttle the process, and resistance from dominant social groups.The logic given for non-implementation is the nature of jobs—that it is technical or research-based. However, in reality such opposition is based on an unwillingness to accept the idea that social representation is and should be an essential concern for an institution. On various occasions, this logic has not only been accepted but also endorsed by various committees or organisations.

It is necessary to highlight that this resistance is far greater in the case of specialised technical and medical education as compared to other institutions. Some of these institutions seek to remain outside the ambit of affirmative action in the name of quality, merit, and autonomy to decide their own policy in recruitments or admissions. Institutions like IIMs or IITs are two such examples. Sidharth Joshi and Deepak Malghan (2017) have highlighted the absence of social diversity in IIMs across the country. Even the state has accepted this logic, as can be seen from the statement of the Veerappa Moily-led oversight committee that submitted its report in 2006 to chalk out a path for smoother implementation of OBC reservations in higher education. The committee in its recommendations highlighted that institutions of global reputationshould be given the autonomy to determine their own rules of recruitment. In other words, they may choose not to implement provisions of reservations:

> The Committee recognizes that those institutions of higher learning which have established a global reputation (e.g. IITs, IIMs, IISc and AIIMS and other such exceptionally exceptional quality institutions) can only maintain that if the highest quality in both faculty and students is ensured. Therefore, the committee recommends that the threshold for admission should be determined by the respective institution alone, as is done today, commensurate with the level of its excellence.[4]

By doing so the committee failed to address the wider question of social representation and inclusivity in these institutions. Such pretexts continue to be used to stall the implementation of reservations, reinforcing entrenched inequality and fostering a homogenous socioeconomic character within academia.

Even in case of student admissions in private universities, institutions violate such norms. Regulatory bodies like UGC are reduced to an advisory role in such matters (R. Sujatha 2020).

NCST data on the number of STs in central universities shows that at the level of full professor, the representation of STs is negligible (0.3 per cent), against the required 7.5 per cent. Major universities including Banaras Hindu University (BHU), University of Delhi (DU), Jamia Milia Islamia (JMI), Hyderabad University and Jawaharlal Nehru University (JNU) did not have a single professor from an ST community in 2013 (NCST 2016: 258). In Group D posts as well, the proportion of STs hired in universities was 2.94 per cent (ibid.). The commission in its reports repeatedly highlighted the problem of dereservation of ST posts into unreserved posts.

The same logic has been deployed in the case of PSUs. Although PSUs are also bound by Government of India regulations, the subject of reservations has not been discussed extensively and they also enjoy a certain degree of autonomy to implement reservation policy as they see fit, in the name of technical expertise requirements. Table 3.6 below shows the dismal state of representation of SCs and OBCs in PSUs under the central government.

Table 3.6: Representation of SCs and OBCs in Public Sector Enterprises (2015–2016)

Groups	*Total employees*	*No of SC employees*	*Percentage of SC employees*	*No of OBC employees*	*Percentage of OBC employees*
A (Managerial/ executive level)	2,62,911	38,539	14.66	34,944	13.29
B (Supervisory level)	1,29,996	14,282	10.99	13,984	10.76
C (Workers skilled)	6,47,511	1,27,839	19.74	1,13,863	17.58
D (Workers unskilled)	2,48,743	40,633	16.33	38,538	15.49
Total	12,89,161	2,21,293	17.16	2,01,329	15.62

Source: NCSC Annual Report (2016: 212).

Institutional and Procedural Challenges

In the previous section we discussed the structural aspects of reservations and the exclusion–discrimination duo. Institutional mechanisms exist at multiple levels to ensure the implementation of reservations. For example, the Department of Personnel and Training (DoPT) is responsible for drawing up guidelines to enable policy compliance. The department updates details about their work at regular intervals; guidelines, policies and other details are available on the website. Apart from the DoPT, national commissions are also statutory bodies meant to oversee implementation. At the micro organisational level, institutional cells responsible for oversight at the level of specific institutions.

Role of Commissions

A major concern for the Constituent Assembly was to ensure that the safeguards provided for the SCs and STs are implemented, and that implementation is monitored. For this purpose, provisions for a Special Commissioner were made in the Constitution under Article 338. When this Article was placed before the Assembly, it was debated at length. Two major issues emerged: (i) the role of the parliament in discussing the report submitted by the commissioner, and (ii) the issue of religious minorities. A third, related issue was the question of including the term 'backward classes' along with the SCs and STs.

Sardar Hukum Singh raised the issue of inclusion of Sikhs from East Pakistan who identified as SCs. He argued that excluding religious minorities from the ambit of the Special Commissioner left religious minorities' concerns unaddressed. K. M. Munshi insisted on the inclusion of Anglo-Indian communities along with SCs and STs (Constitutional Assembly debates 1949b). The issue was discussed on 26 August 1949. Ambedkar, explaining why minorities were not covered in Article 388, highlighted that the representatives of the Sikh and Muslim communities had agreed that they should not be considered as minorities for the purpose of affirmative action. Hence, the only groups covered were the SCs, STs and Anglo-Indian communities (Constitutional Assembly debates 1949a).

The Constitution-makers had thus inserted special provisions to oversee implementation of reservation in the central government services. However, till the end of twentieth century the office of commissioner was merely a bureaucratic body whose emphasis was mainly the collection of data related to implementation of reservations. The office did not play a role in ensuring effective or faster implementation.

Though the DoPT is responsible for drawing guidelines for reservations, its ambit was restricted to the central government recruitments. It wasn't in a position to monitor the autonomous institutions or state government institutions for this purpose. However, with the increasing responsibilities with regard to the issue of social justice and implementation of these provisions it was realised that a commissioner's office was not adequate to ensure the effective implementation.

In 1978, it was realised that one commissioner may not be enough to protect the interests of the Scheduled Castes across the country. Hence, a multi-member commission along with the commissioner's office was established through a government resolution. The statutory National Commission for SCs & STs came into being on 12 March 1992 through the 65th Constitutional Amendment Act, 1990. This amendment replaced the Special Commissioners' Office.

Subsequently, this body was replaced in the 89th Constitution Amendment Act, 2003 as per a notification dated 19 February 2004. The erstwhile National Commission for SCs & STs was replaced with two separate commissions: the National Commission for Scheduled Castes (NCSC), and the National Commission for Scheduled Tribes (NCST).[5] This was based on the recognition that the issues faced by the two groups were very different, and that clubbing both of them under one commission would lead to a neglect of the concerns of people from the Scheduled Tribes. Both commissions were made responsible for the effective implementation of constitutional safeguards meant for the respective groups. Besides, the commissionalso had a responsibility to ensure socioeconomic development of marginalised groups and address grievances of these communities. To ensure that commissions can perform their duties freely, special safeguards were provided.

The 89th Amendment Act provides judicial powers to the NCSC, allowing it to enquire into any case of discrimination, harassment, or atrocity against members of the Scheduled Castes anywhere in the country. In addition, both commissions were also given the power to inquire into matters related to the functioning of institutional safeguards meant to ensure that members of SC communities are able to access constitutional entitlements. Another aspect of their work was contributing to the planning process with measures specifically designed to promote welfare of the two groups.

How the commission has evolved as an institution is best observed by looking at the annual reports available on its website. The commission reports are a great repository on the issue of discrimination of marginalised groups. These reports also highlight various loopholes in the state policy with regard to addressing the concerns of marginalisation and discrimination. Above all, various reports also detail the status of state policies in terms of achieving their targets for the welfare of SC, ST and OBC communities.[6]

Unlike the NCSC, the NCST was seen as a body responsible for ensuring overall development of ST communities as well as good governance of Scheduled areas. The NCST has the following functions as per the Clause 5 of Article 338A:

1. To investigate & monitor matters relating to Safeguards provided for STs under the Constitution or under other laws or under Govt. Order, to evaluate the working of such Safeguards.

2. To inquire into specific complaints relating to Rights & Safeguards of STs;
3. To participate and advise in the Planning Process relating to Socio-economic development of STs, and to evaluate the progress of their development under the Union and any State;
4. To submit report to the President annually and at such other times as the Commission may deem fit, upon/ working of Safeguards, measures required for effective implementation of Programmers/ Schemes relating to Welfare and Socio-economic development of STs;
5. To discharge such other functions in relation to STs as the President may, subject to the provisions of any law made by Parliament, by rule specify;
6. The Commission would also discharge the following other functions in relation to the protection, welfare and development & advancement of the Scheduled Tribes, namely:-
   i. Measures that need to be taken over conferring ownership rights in respect of minor forest produce to the Scheduled Tribes living in forest areas.
   ii. Measures to be taken to safeguard rights to the Tribal Communities over mineral resources, water resources etc. as per law.
   iii. Measures to be taken for the development of tribals and to work for move viable livelihood strategies.
   iv. Measures to be taken to improve the efficacy of relief and rehabilitation measures for tribal groups displaced by development projects.
   v. Measures to be taken to prevent alienation of tribal people from land and to effectively rehabilitate such

people in whose case alienation has already taken place.

vi. Measures to be taken to elicit maximum cooperation and involvement of Tribal Communities for protecting forests and undertaking social afforestation.

vii. Measures to be taken to ensure full implementation of the Provisions of Panchayats (Extension to the Scheduled Areas) Act, 1996 (40 of 1996).

viii. Measures to be taken to reduce and ultimately eliminate the practice of shifting cultivation by Tribals that lead to their continuous disempowerment and degradation of land and the environment.

Policy-makers soon realised that a similar body was also required to safeguard the interests of the Backward Classes and a national commission for the backward classes was constituted through an executive order in 1993. The National Commission for Backward Classes (NCBC) was initially constituted by the Central Govt by the National Commission for Backward Classes Act, 1993 (27 of 1993) dated 2 April 1993.[7] However, since the commission had to be empowered with various functions like the NCSC and NCST, the Constitution (One Hundred and Second Amendment) Act, 2018 was passed by Parliament. Through this amendment, Article 338B was inserted in the Constitution, making the NCBC a statutory body. The Commission consists of a chairperson, vice-chairperson and three other members of the rank and pay of secretary to the GoI and their condition of service and tenure of office has been notified vide a Ministry of Social Justice and Empowerment notification dated 23 August 2018.

The functions of the NCBC are similar to the other two commissions, whereby it has the power to investigate and monitor implementation of various safeguards provided in the Constitution for the socially and economically backward sections. Besides, the commission can inquire into complaints regarding violation of such measures. The commission can suggest measures to be taken for the upliftment of such sections.

Importantly, apart from addressing concerns raised by various individuals and groups regarding, the commission also provides analyses of various government policies, especially in terms of service-related safeguards, including reservations.

Since the NCBC is a new commission, it is still in the process of evolution. Reports on the status of OBCs are also compiled by various state governments. Discussions connected to the central government OBC list are relatively few on the NCBC website. The commission could notify its rules of operations only in late 2020, after the national lockdown declared in the wake of the Covid-19 pandemic ended. In recent times, the commission seems to be taking up issues in a proactive manner, but it still has a long way to go.

The other two commissions on the other hand have developed themselves as effective institutional bodies. The reports of the NCSC and NCST concerning the condition of SC/ST communities in various socioeconomic spheres are very detailed. They also provide details data on the number of people in services in each state or various services.

The NCBC appears to be dealing only with routine bureaucratic matters like provisions, bills, grants for its functioning, etc. The only major work undertaken by the commission so far is the question of inclusion of various groups in the OBC list. The commission has provided a detailed account of socioeducational conditions of various groups who are demanding to be included in the OBC list.

In case of the NCSC and NCST, the annual reports are full of information and action taken by these institutional bodies. On the contrary, the NCBC, as mentioned earlier, seems to be struggling with its existence. Since its constitutional status was notified in 2018 and its formal rules of functioning were adopted in the year 2020, the commission is yet to find a more effective *modus operandi*. So far, the reports of the commission appear to be merely bureaucratic records and compilation of action taken reports providing constitutional provisions and tables indicating day-to-day expenditures incurred by its activities.

The NCBC commission also does not look at the socioeconomic status of various castes defined as the OBC unlike the two other commissions which spend majority of its time in mapping these developmental indicators. Reports of the NCSC and NCST are full of analysis of various schemes meant for development of these social groups, their progress and above all the challenges faced by these groups. These reports also map various ways in which discrimination and exclusion takes place and how various institutional safeguards can be introduced or existing mechanisms can be strengthened. The OBC commission provides no such information in its annual reports. There is no data available on the NCBC website dealing with the socioeconomic conditions or implementation of service safeguards in the form of affirmative action.

Despite their financial or organisational institutions, the three commissions do have a major role to play in empowering various intra-institutional mechanisms which are in place to look into grievances of various individuals working in different institutions. The SC/ST cells, or liaison officers who are the real eyes and ears of the commissions in each of the institutions, bank on the commissions for final and effective intervention in violation of various rules or protection of interests of these marginalised social groups.

Role of Liaison Officers

The liaison officer is a critical link in the larger apparatus for ensuring fair implementation of reservations. In the case of recruitments in various ministries and departments, the concerned ministry provides details of their liaison officers. It states that the liaison officer should be at the rank of deputy secretary. They shall bear the responsibility to supervise the maintenance of the roster register and reservation register. In case the officer finds any discrepancy in implementation, it should be brought to the notice of the head of the institution. It is the responsibility of the head of the institution to take action in this regard and rectify the problem.

These clauses sound very simple and the role of liaison appears to be extremely critical. Yet, in reality, the office of the liaison officer is a powerless institution.[8] The liaisons work under tremendous political pressure and also pressure from the head of the institutions to clear the roster and reservation roster. This is partly because job promotions of liaison officers themselves, like those of other employees, are contingent on the favour of the head of the institution. In such circumstances, no liaison would be willing to displease the institutional head by pointing out problems in the roster points or reservation points.Thus, the post of the liaison officer becomes mired in questions of 'loyalty' to the head of the institution. Generally, the post is prone to biased appointments to ensure that the liason does not raise questions about the recruitments.

Liaison are usually also tagged as 'doing caste politics' or exhibiting caste bias if they raise issues related to roster points. They are also blamed for 'holding up' appointments if they flag problems in the roster points or in reservation register. Such problems are more frequent in the case of autonomous institutions/ bodies in the Government of India or in the state governments.

As a result of such pressures, the liaison officer is reduced to simply a rubber stamp. Liaisons are not granted any protection against unfair punitive measures that could enable them to perform their task independently, without any fear of authority. Further, they are not provided with enough resources either and are asked to work out the roster themselves in case of any issues.

There are hardly any efforts on the part of governments to train members of various marginalised communities about the nuances of reservation policy. Consequently, most officers are largely ignorant about the policy and its implementation. They mainly bank on the other senior officers to learnt about such complexities. Besides, most of the documents available on the website are technically so complex that for an ordinary member it may not be possible to understand the process so easily.

Intra-institutional Mechanisms: SC–ST–OBC Cell

The SC–ST cells are intra-institutional bodies formed to create awareness among students, candidates or other employees from reserved categories about their rights as stipulated in the Constitution of India. Besides, the cells also work as grievance redressal mechanisms for the communities. These bodies received special support from the University Grants Commission (UGC) and All India Council for Technical Education (AICTE). During the Tenth Five Year Plan period, the union government laid special emphasis on strengthening these bodies in institutions for higher education. It was mandatory for all colleges and universities to have such a cell. The SC/ST cells are also responsible for providing support to students in various academic institutions. It organises talks and seminars to sensitise students and faculty and foster awareness about its role. The UGC, through its guidelines, has made SC/ST cells mandatory and clearly delineated its functions:[9]

1. To implement the reservation policy for SCs/STs in the Universities and Colleges.
2. To collect data regarding the implementation of the policies in respect of admissions, appointments to teaching and non-teaching positions in the universities, and in the affiliating colleges and analyse the data showing the trends and changes towards fulfilling the required quota.
3. To take such follow up measures for achieving the objectives and targets laid down for the purpose by the Government of India and the UGC.
4. To implement, monitor and evaluate continuously the reservation policy in universities and colleges and plan measures for ensuring effective implementation of the policy and programme of the Government of India.

During the Tenth plan for Higher Education, the UGC had put special emphasis on the formation of such cells. The UGC had also provided special funds for this purpose. A major function of the cell is to ensure that the reservation policy is implemented in educational institutions.

At the micro-institutional level, the formation of such committees was a very effective step. It provided an opportunity and space to teachers, students and administrative staff of marginalised sections to freely intervene in the institutional matters. They could ensure that representation was provided to students and teachers coming from marginalised sections. Due to their accessibility, they can play a crucial role in preventing everyday harassment on the basis of caste. The availability of such bodies within institutions was a major step towards better redressal.

However, much like other institutional mechanisms, the SC/ST cell also suffers from bureaucratic hassles and other pressures. The cells are overburdened with extra tasks, and in most institutes the cell acts only when there is a formal complaint from a student or employee. Cell representatives are less keen on taking proactive initiatives as this may lead to conflict. Besides, quite like the liaison officers, SC/ST cell representatives are under constant pressure and do not have autonomy or employment safeguards, making them vulnerable to persecution.[10] These cells must also contend with complaints from institutions that their work does not directly add to the institution. In such an atmosphere, even representatives may be unaware of their responsibilities and inclined to view these cells as mere bureaucratic bodies for grievance redressal. Thus, despite their potential, SC/ST cells have not been able to live up to their objectives, functions and relevance.

The Reservation Roster

A major policy tool for the implementation of reservations is the roster. Regular maintenance of both reservation register and roster register is a prerequisite for transparency and accountability in creating a representative recruitment process. The DoPT guidelines categorically state that a roster register should be maintained by every ministry, department, or concerned institution. The reservation roster should be verified by the liaison officer periodically.

However, in many institutions the roster registers are not maintained properly and are prepared only during recruitment. This is often observed in institutions where recruitment does not take place regularly, including academic and autonomous institutions. Administrative staff often lacks training to maintain such registers. Hence, a temporary or ad hoc mechanism is typically in use, and the registers are not available for public scrutiny. Thus, even though roster points are not a secret document, most institutions fail to maintain transparency in keeping records such documents. This is the reason that appointments are frequently embroiled in litigation, leading to delays in recruitment.

As highlighted earlier, discrepancies highlighted by the concerned liaison officer are seen as attempts to stall the process of recruitment. These conflicts lead to further delays, eventually creating a backlog of vacant positions and further aggravating the grievances of those who are not covered in the reservation policy.

Another major issue is the question of roster point. Due to non-maintenance of data of employees, institutions sometimes change the roster points of their retired employees. This creates complications in implementation of reservations. Any change in the roster point may alter the nature of position to be advertised and whether it would be reserved or unreserved. For instance, an important debate took place recently on the question of institution or department-level reservation and the 200-point roster. The Supreme Court in one of its judgements allowed departments within institutions to be considered a 'unit' for allocating reserved seats, deviating from established practice. This was popularly termed the '13-point roster'. Various civil society organisations opposed this move as it would have resulted in a decline in the total number of reserved positions. This debate was settled when the Government of India introduced legislation to implement reservations at the level of the institution, thereby overriding the controversial court ruling (Penkar 2019; Ram and Mann 2019).

These mechanisms have changed over time. Till 1997, reservation was determined at the level of specific vacancies. In the R. K. Sabharwal v. State of Punjab Case, the Supreme Court ruled that reservation should be implemented on the basis of number of posts per cadre and not on vacancies alone. This resulted in a major shortfall of reserved vacancies filled. Accordingly, post-based reservation was adopted on 2 July 1997. With this new provision, an exchange of posts between different reserved categories, for instance between SC and ST seats, was no longer possible. Post-based reservation rules stated the once a post was reserved, it would stay in that particular category unless a process of dereservation was followed.

The Data Challenge and Debate on Caste Census

A major challenge in implementation of reservation policy is the lack of regular, consistent data for a wider period and covering the whole country. Despite the fact that India has multiple layers of discrimination and exclusion, there is no consistency of data on these indicators. Though caste is regarded as the most important variable in policy on affirmative action, the last caste census that enumerated the population of different caste categories in India and their developmental indicators was conducted almost eight decades ago in 1931. It was this caste census that determined caste-based affirmative action policies. It was only in 2011 that the government again conducted a socioeconomic and caste census with multiple indicators of measuring backwardness. However, the data was never made public in its entirety.

In 2021, when the demands for a fresh caste census erupted once again, the Bihar state government supported the demand. The government of Maharashtra filed a PIL in the Supreme Court demanding that the central government be directed to conduct a caste census along with the regular decadal census. The union government opposed this request. In the affidavit, the central government highlighted that the 2011 caste data was rife with data-collection anomalies and that the classification of backward classes was also problematic. Taking these technical difficulties into account, the government had decided not to make the 2011 data public, nor did it come up with any plan for caste census.

Proposing a different affirmative action policy model that could cover a wide range of indicators of backwardness and not merely caste, Satish Deshpande and Yogendra Yadav argued for an an evidence-based affirmative action policy (Deshpande and Yadav 2006). However, what makes it difficult to reach out to substantive conclusion is the lack of regularly published data with wider coverage:

> By an evidence-based approach we mean a policy framework that is explicitly linked to empirical information relating to disadvantage, usually but not necessarily of a macro-statistical kind. The major advantage of such an approach is that it highlights the fundamental reasons why affirmative action is being undertaken—namely, various sorts of social and economic disadvantage. This helps to de-essentialise identity markers like caste or religion—i.e. it provides a rational explanation why specific castes or communities are entitled to compensatory discrimination and undermines attitudes that treat such entitlements as a 'birthright'. (ibid.: 2420)

Maintaining data pertaining to a highly differentiated caste system does pose a challenge. However, the onus is on the government to develop mechanisms to gather regular, credible data on the status of various caste groups in India. A more coordinated federal system needs to be put in place for this purpose. Data on caste is not only about reservations, but also about making overall policymaking in India more people-centric. For instance, Suthar (2018) discusses the relevance of caste data to policies meant to tackle the problem of droughts.

Summing Up

This chapter highlighted some of the challenges of implementation of reservation policy, the available institutional mechanisms and the structural factors that play an outsized role in this process. The 1990s saw shifts in the implementation of reservations, discourses on vacant positions, and the introduction of new rules required for the fulfilment of reserved quotas. However, India also witnessed major social and economic transformations in this decade that led to emergence of a new kind of politics around these issues. The new economic policy of liberalisation allowed the private sector a greater share of economic activity, taking over sectors that were otherwise reserved for the state. These reforms would come to determine the nature of debate around reservations that unfolded in the 2000s.

Notes

1. A major reason behind this was the Supreme Court's decision to place a 50 per cent cap on reservations. Any expansion of reservation was considered as an encroachment on the share of previously defined marginalised groups.

2. A few examples in this context can be cited. One is of a Dalit teacher's experience of harassment by faculty colleagues in IIT Kanpur (*Firstpost* 2018); another is a case from IIT Madras (*Vox Populi* 2022).

3. In her PhD dissertation, Shambhavi Sahai discusses discrimination that she witnessed in a workshop meant for training the teachers. See Sahai (2018).

4. Report available at http://www.academics-india.com/moily%20report.pdf (accessed May 2024).

5. See https://www.ncst.nic.in/sites/default/files/documents/constitutional_amendments/844.pdf (accessed May 2024).

6. See https://dopt.gov.in/policy-reservation-scs-sts-and-obcs (accessed May 2024).

7. See https://indiankanoon.org/doc/637725/ (accessed August 2024).

8. These descriptions are based on discussions with liaison officers who have worked in academic institutions.

9. See https://www.ugc.ac.in/oldpdf/xplanpdf/special_cell.pdf (accessed August 2024).

10. This section is based on the authors' own observations of the functioning of these cells in different institutions, especially in universities and colleges.

four

Neoliberal Economic Reforms and Reservations

This chapter looks at the changing domestic context post the initiation of structural economic reforms in the 1990s. These reforms were implemented in a changing socioeconomic and political context. Significantly, they have shaped recent debates around affirmative action in India and will presumably continue to inform public opinion. This chapter shows how the rise of the 'new middle class' has redefined the debate on affirmative action, leading to the introduction of reservations based solely on economic criteria, that is, the introduction of the EWS category.

Structural Reforms and Neoliberalism in India

The arrival of neoliberal economic policies in India is seen as a major policy shift from a state-oriented, regulated developmental paradigm to a market-centric economic model. Generally, the tenure of the Congress government in 1991–1996, led by Prime Minister P. V. Narsimha Rao, which introduced deregulation of key economic sectors controlled by the state, is considered to be the starting point of neoliberal economic policies in India. With this new economic policy coming in, the policy of reservations in India also witnessed a major shift.

Generally, the debate on neoliberalism and its social implications ignores the background of the 1980s, which witnessed the adoption of recommendations made by the Mandal Commission (as discussed in Chapter 2). It is essential to remember that this policy shift in favour of the backward classes was not the starting point for OBC politics in various states, especially those in North India. It was actually the reverse. In the face of emerging political consolidation of the OBCs, and the denial of political opportunity to them by the Congress-ruled government, other parties—especially Janata Dal—decided to woo OBCs by extending the benefits of reservation. Though the debate regarding reservation for backward communities was already underway by the 1980s, it was not taken up seriously until former Prime Minister V. P. Singh decided to implement the Mandal Commission Report.

The implementation of Mandal Commission Report faced backlash almost from all sections including bureaucrats, academicians, and politicians. In an interesting analysis, renowned economist Dharma Kumar (1992) discusses various criteria used by the Mandal Commission to identify social backwardness. However, the sources used to question the relevance of reservations in the government sector or various educational institutions are not very convincing or adequate. The only significant finding that the author cites is a newspaper article published in *The Indian Express*, which quoted a study and reported that accidents in the railways were connected with declining morale of the staff, and which in turn identified the implementation of reservations as the only cause of this declining morale. The other two broad arguments used by Kumar are: (i) once implemented, reservations cannot be withdrawn, and; (ii) the list of castes included will continue to increase. The author fails to show the problem associated with the two points. It is assumed that reservation in itself is a problem and hence its continuation is a problem.

K. C. Suri (1995) had speculated that implementation of reservation policy may lead to rising conflicts amongst various caste groups. However, he also explains that growing conflicts are more an outcome of the fears of the upper-caste poor and urban middle-classes that they would not be able to 'catch up' with reserved category candidates in education and jobs. This created a sense of being the 'loser' in the policy, leading to conflicts. Taken together with the arguments made by Dharma Kumar (1992), the only way to prevent such conflicts would be by allowing the status quo to be maintained. The only method to overcome such situations, Suri argues, is by building a new consensus amongst political parties where the concerns of social justice are addressed in a more meaningful and substantial sense (Suri 1995: 231).

Besides, the claim about a link between railways accidents and the implementation of reservation, which was prominently featured in reportage at the time, was strongly refuted by a later study that analysed the performance of the Indian railways vis-à-vis reservation for SC and ST employees. An econometric analysis by Ashwini Deshpande and Thomas E. Weisskopf (2014) showed that since the 1980s, accidents declined continuously. Hence, it is not plausible to argue that implementation of reservations hampers sectoral productivity. On the contrary, by using time series data for railway output and employees from SC/ST categories as an input factor, the two authors argue that there is a positive correlation between the two variables. In other words, the increase in employees from SC/ST communities (owing to better implementation of reservations) has positively impacted its productivity.

It was immediately after the implementation of the Mandal Commission Report that the economic reforms for liberalisation were introduced. The implementation of these reforms pushed the debate on issues of social justice and representation in new directions by bringing in the issues of efficiency or what is popularly referred to as 'merit'. It is not that these issues were not at the forefront prior to this period. However, the logic of efficiency and merit brought a new vocabulary into public discourse and was linked with the entry of private players in various economic sectors.

The question of administrative efficiency was already being deliberated during the 1980s with the discussion on the question of administrative efficiency in India. During the Seventh and Eighth Five-Year Plans, a special focus was on the role of administrative machinery in implementing various policies and concerns about prevailing nepotism and corruption. Amidst this, when the implementation of Mandal Commission Report was announced, the logic of efficiency was used as a tool to counter the issue of social justice and representation. Representation was seen as a policy tool that would negatively impact the administrative efficiency of the state.

In the early 1990s, Atul Kohli's (1991) famous coinage of 'crisis of governability' raised concerns about the Indian state's ability to implement various social welfare policies and ensure law and order. Kohli claimed that efficient bureaucrats in the southern states had helped them achieve greater human development and policy efficiency compared to the rest of India.

Not only locally but also at the global level, the implicit logic of efficiency was becoming a dominant popular narrative. The World Bank's idea of 'good governance' focused on whether conditions were suitable for the functioning of the market, and efficiency was a major qualitative indicator for their assessment (Jayal 1997). The rise of the East Asian 'tiger' economies due to increasing flows of foreign direct investment (FDI) and the expanding role of private players in their economies was projected as a major indicator of growth and development and a model to be emulated.

In the field of education, too, the logic of efficiency was used to counter the question of representation of various caste groups. Educational institutions have in fact been a major site of contestation in the case of reservation policy. A major reason for this is the legacy of the colonial era, where education emerged as a tool enabling exposure to modernity and opened up new forms of socioeconomic mobility. A majority of the beneficiaries of colonial-era education were from the upper castes. By virtue of this generational advantage, they continued to have a disproportionately high presence in various state institutions after independence. Reservations opened up such closed educational spaces to students coming from marginalised groups. However, this was projected by dominant castes as an attempt to harm the principle of 'merit' in such institutions. Technical institutions like IITs have begun implementing reservations in appointments and admissions fairly recently, and IIMs remain beyond reservation policy purview.

Ajantha Subramanian argues how, in case of IITs, the logic of merit was used to perpetuate prevailing social hierarchies:

> The majority of IITians come from upper-caste families of bureaucrats, schoolteachers, and academics, where capital has long been held in education. While arguably from middle-class backgrounds, the value of their accumulated 'caste capital' has suddenly spiked due to the reorganization of late twentieth- and early twenty-first-century capitalism around the 'knowledge economy.' At the same time, the role of caste and state in producing IITians has been obscured in favor of their portrayal as uniquely meritorious individuals. (Subramanian 2019: 7)

She further explains how this interplay between caste and modernity gets rearticulated by the logic of merit. Meritocracy in this sense is not a tool of democratisation or empowerment. Rather, it further exacerbates inequalities. Within IITs, for example, the state attempt to ensure representation of marginalised groups in its various programmes was met with a backlash in the form of 'reservation-based discrimination' of students belonging to the SC, ST, or OBC communities (see the discussion in Chapter 2). In a qualitative study of one such institution, Anupam Joya Sharma and Malavika Subramanyam showed how the stigmatisation of reservation policy has further impacted students psychologically, putting them in high-stress situations dominated by 'fear of failure, academic disinterest and low self-esteem' (Sharma and Subramanyam 2020: 9). The upper caste students on the other hand, owing to their own frustrations, target students coming from weaker sections. This psychological toll is reflected in the worrying number of suicide deaths of students belonging to marginalised groups.

The New Indian Middle Class

By the middle of the 1990s, the Indian labour market started looking very different compared to the 1980s. An increasing share of service sector, especially white collar jobs in technology companies based in metropolitan cities like Bangalore and Hyderabad were major drivers of change. As per the Economic Survey of India 2023–24, the service sector's contribution to the country's Gross Domestic Product (GDP) skyrocketed, with a majority of this share belonged to various technology firms. Leela Fernandes (2006), in her work on the Indian middle class, has argued that this economic change was reflected in sociocultural change among the new middle classes of India. Despite their increasing wealth, a sense of structural as well as cultural differentiation was embedded in these groups. The new middle class was not free of the traditional caste baggage of Indian society. Fernandes also explains how this new middle class was required to participate in a new cultural lifestyle and generate new forms of social capital for itself in order to be a part of a new 'corporatised' lifestyle characteristic of technology and finance firms. Explaining the new caste-class intersections that thus emerged, she argues:

> ...this intersection of caste and class is being intensified in the construction of the new liberalizing middle class. While changing patterns of white-collar employment and the entry of lower caste groups into the middle classes has been aided by state affirmative action policies and state employment, the private sector has been outside the purview of such policies. The social differentiation that has taken root within middle class government jobs has occurred as the status of middle-class employment has been shifting from state to private-sector jobs. (Fernandes 2006: 104)

She further explains that the story of this new middle class was not only an economic story. Rather, it was also about the formation of a new cultural identity that was deeply connected with a restructuring of urban spaces. This was also about 'purification' of the urban public space, with a new sense of aesthetics, security, and social character (Fernandes 2006: 139). The formation of this identity was closely linked with the caste identity of this middle class, which had developed a new social outlook and consumption patterns and yet remained deeply embedded in its caste background. In other words, the new economy and middle class reinvented traditional forms of exclusion in these redesigned urban spaces.

The middle class that emerged after the 1990s was qualitatively different from the middle class of other historical phases in India. The colonial middle class had been a product of the British education system and worked for the colonial government and its ethos. It was deeply embedded in rural social structures, since it largely comprised the landed elites who could harness colonial education and government employ to support their middle class identity and lifestyle. The middle class of 1960s and 1970s was a product of the Indian economic initiatives, especially the Nehruvian modernisation drive. Sociologically, it was different from the colonial middle class, but economically it too was supported by the government sector, which offered a wide range of employment opportunities. The middle class of 1990s was thus qualitatively different as it was a product of the privatisation and corporatisation. Besides, it was also deeply embedded in the new urban culture that was emerging in India, and influenced by a burgeoning consumerist culture.

Another important influence was the non-resident Indian (NRI) community that had settled in the countries of North America, UK, and Australia. The NRIs were still embedded in India's culture as well as economy and left a great imprint on the newly emerging middle class in the 1980s. The increasing influence of Indian diasporia resulted in increasing aspirations of the Indian middle class. Shrayana Bhattacharya's insightful description of the new middle class being drawn to the persona of Shah Rukh Khan in Bollywood movies of the 1990s, whose imaginary heavily featured Western countries, sheds light on these processes (Bhattacharya 2021). Technocrats and software engineers who had trained in India and began migrating to the US were hailed as success stories of market-led growth in the Western world. These stories also became a reference point for comparative judgements about the poor state of affairs in India. These stories also came along with their implicit biases, since privatisation played a major role in the development of the European and North American countries. The Silicon Valley boom, which attracted many young professionals from India, was also a carrier of such stories of modernisation that were missing in Indian cities and the countryside.

In effect, changing domestic conditions and a global narrative of growth, development, and modernisation had a great deal of influence on the Indian middle class. The new middle class that was rising by the 1980s was more conscious of these changing conditions and also aspirational. These middle-class aspirations were about getting access to education (especially technical and medical education), and also an access to the government sector jobs. It was also about achieving a 'West-like modernisation' of public services. It was also about demands for the creation of a new market-based model of development which should be free of any 'caste-based discrimination such as reservations' and should be exclusively based on 'quality' and 'merit'. This new middle class was largely composed of upper castes; further, its aspirations did not imply an understanding of the historical conditions of the 'West'. For it, the 'West' was its highways, malls, and bright colours, and all that was missing in India. The reservation policy was seen as a major deterrent to such developments.

The new model of development was focused on the expansion of the private sector into new domains, especially the service sector. It questioned the relevance of PSUs and their inability in providing public services in an efficient manner. It was this changing local as well as global context that gave rise to a new debate in India that questioned the relevance of prevailing model of development and welfarism. The question of efficiency was seen as a natural corollary of such a debate. Amidst this, the entire debate about affirmative action shifted to a logic of merit, at the expense of larger questions of social justice, welfarism, the state's responsibility towards empowerment of marginalised communities, and democratisation in the sense of representation.

The private sector was seen as an alternative to public sector enterprises. It was also projected as a more 'secular' and 'equal' sector where only efficiency and merit were to be the criteria and not any other parameter such as caste. This led to the emergence of a new debate regarding reservation for marginalised groups in the private sector.

Beyond from the fact that the new middle class had a class as well as caste character, it was not a homogenous category. There were internal differentiations within the middle class, with different strands expressing different notions of welfarism, the role of the state, and state policy. The new debate was also about a 'Dalit middle class' or a 'Muslim middle class', etc. (Jodhka and Prakash 2016). While the upper-caste middle class was speaking against welfarism and defending a free market as a solution to socioeconomic problems, the Dalit middle class was articulating a different position on these issues. It was demanding a shift in the policy by expanding the safeguards available in public sector employment to the private sector as well. By the late 1990s, this demand took a new form with the articulation of a demand to implement of reservations in the private sector.

Debates on Reservations in the Private Sector

By the end of the twentieth century, with five decades of reservation policy, a new group among the Scheduled Castes and Other Backward Classes had emerged. This class was now in a position to assert its demands in a very effective manner. Quite like the upper castes in colonial India who were introduced to modernity through the colonial education system, a section of various socially marginalised groups also found access to modernity and its urban character.

With the implementation of neoliberal economic reforms, this group was conscious that the new economic reforms are going to change the character of Indian economy and society. With the decline in state investment in organised sector employment and gradual rise of the Indian technical force concentrated in the private sector, this section was aware that the policy of reservation will gradually become irrelevant. Hence, they began to articulate demands for representation in the private sector through affirmative action policy.

In the 1990s, there were demands for extending reservation for the marginalised communities in the private sector employment as well (Thorat et al. 2005). The rise of service sector, especially telecommunication sector has provided plenty of job opportunities in the private sector.

In the year 2006 when the UPA government was in power, a coordination committee was set up to initiate formal dialogue on this subject with the representative bodies of Indian industries. This panel included FICCI and CII. The industry vehemently opposed such efforts. Sunil Kumar Munjal, president of CII, opposed the move by arguing that:

> We cannot be forced to take individuals who do not have the required skills. We cannot afford to compromise on efficiency. That would affect our competitiveness. We cannot compromise on merit. Corporate sector doesn't go by the colour of skin, caste or the last name. (Quoted in Thimmaiah 2005: 747)

Such reactions were based on the assumption that skills, efficiency, and competitiveness are closely associated with few castes and representation of others would be to the detriment of all these factors. However, a few industrialists such as Ratan Tata responded positively:

> Tata group certainly understands the social responsibility that all industries should carry to bring social justice to SC/ST and other minority or underprivileged sections of our community. We would be happy to support your initiative. (Quoted in Thimmaiah 2005: 747)

This encouraged the UPA government to proactively pursue the issue. A parliamentary panel during UPA-I called for a comprehensive legislation to ensure representation of marginalised groups in the private sector. The panel highlighted that merely having voluntary measures may not be a feasible policy for the purpose of achieving social equality. The parliamentary panel highlighted this by citing other reports of the Government of India:

> .... Affirmative action such as working towards skill formation, scholarship and training of the weaker sections of the society which the private industry willing to undertake, does not appear to be sufficient. The committee strongly feels that only legislation on reservations would guarantee employment for SCs and STs in private sector with which the government also agrees. (Ramachandran 2006)

Caste discrimination was not confined to rural structures or public institutions, as was widely believed. Instead, scholars at this time had begun to show that caste discrimination had changed its face in view of urbanisation and changing economic realities. Exclusion, in this sense, was also getting 'modernised'. Rise of the private sector was not a guarantee of fairness in the market as was widely propagated.

Sukhdeo Thorat and Paul Attewell (2007) argued in a study that in case of private sector, discrimination occurs right at the outset. Through a methodology that involved applying for various posts advertised in the private sector, the authors showed that surnames/titles that denote belonging to particular caste or religious groups are a strong determinant of their being called for an interview. They argued:

> This field experiment study of job applications observed a statistically significant pattern by which, on average, college-educated lower-caste and Muslim job applications fare less well than equivalently-qualified applicants with high caste names, when applying by mail for employment in the modern private-enterprise sector. (Thorat and Attewell 2007: 4144)

According to a press release issued by the government, in its various meetings the industry representatives highlighted that reservation is not a solution to the problem of caste bias. Representatives also opposed any mandatory clause by the government for quotas in recruitment. However, they expressed their willingness to take initiatives to coordinate with the government in introducing and implementing skill development programmes for marginalised groups. The industry also favoured a voluntary code of conduct (VCC) that could be applicable for all the industries.[1] In addition, the industries also agreed to provide more fellowships and other forms of support to those from marginalised sections in order to promote education among them.

However, many believe that the private sector is not free of caste-based discrimination and bias. A news report published in 2019 had shown the grim state of affairs when it comes to the issue of adoption of the VCC by various industries. Out of the 17,788 member companies, just about 19 per cent have adopted the 'voluntary code of conduct for affirmative action' (Khan 2019).

In another report by the *State of Working India*, researchers at Azim Premji University (2023) highlighted that SCs and STs are under-represented in government jobs overall but over-represented in the lower-class government jobs.

As suggested earlier, the reservation debate in this decade witnessed a qualitative shift. This shift occurred due to two reasons. For one, the focus was more on debates surrounding engineering and medical college admissions, which were seen as launch pads for the aspirational, upper-caste middle classes. In post-independence India, a major focus was on the promotion of engineering institutions. IITs being the most prestigious institutions attracted attention of intermediary caste groups. Their interest was bolstered by the fact that IITs enabled access to a lucrative, globalised job market, and that graduates from these institutions were getting well-paid jobs in private firms in the US and Europe. Economically, this was a far better deal than what similar employment could yield in India. In other words, admission in IIT or in any good engineering college was potentially life-changing and could provide economic mobility to whole families. Losing out on admission into such spaces, for any reason, amounted to the collapse of a dream. Similarly, the medical profession was highly lucrative in terms of economic development. India was witnessing a massive demand for medical professionals across the country. It was also a well-recognised, prestigious profession. Anti-reservation attitudes vis-à-vis both these professions were more about defending middle class aspirations than about questions of quality or merit or any social concern.

The second reason had more to do with a misplaced debate on reservations, guided by the logic of economy. Bertrand et al. (2010) studied around 700 households of students seeking admissions to engineering colleges—those who could make it and those who failed to get admission. In the section describing their methods, the authors stated that they asked respondents a question: whom did affirmative action target? They identified two reasons for affirmative action policy: social and economic. They further highlighted a common refrain in the debate on reservations in India: 'Many are afraid that only rich minorities are being helped by the program and, even worse, that rich minorities are displacing poor members of the upper caste' (ibid.: 21). Such descriptions may provide a very convincing economic logic in favour or against reservations but what they tend to ignore is the social context.

In economic descriptions, the question of representation is not even brought into the fray. Such conclusions even ignore the very basic question of representation as being the foremost criteria for having reservations in the first place. In analyses of India's reservation system published abroad, problematic attitudes often emerge that underestimate the problems posed by lack of representation, both in India as well as in Western countries—like the US—that are discussed as having alternative models. Inadequate representation of African-Americans and other minorities in various institutions is also understood from an economic cost-benefit perspective. A similar yardstick is also being used for understanding the Indian conditions. Consequently, the debate shifts and economic criteria becomes a defining logic in itself while larger concerns are sidelined. This became clear when using the same logic, the government decided to introduce reservation for economically weaker sections. As the section below shows, this kind of reservation also took away seats of the upper castes. The upper caste candidates who were already in an employment were displaced since the government policy altered the existing unreserved positions. The government did not declare any intention of increasing the number of seats in various educational institutions. Besides, in case of employment also the government did not bring in any enhancement.

Ironically, the logic of individualistic economic representation was used for implementation of EWS reservation, whereas in highlighting problems with the policy of caste-based reservations the logic of substantive representation or economic backwardness was not given priority. Owing to the same reason, the issue of women's representation has not yet made its way into admission criteria in academic institutions or employment. The lack of regional representation is another question that is being neglected. The logic of group representation is used to do away with logic of economy and vice versa. It ignores the fact that the logic of representation and economy has to go hand in hand.

The political fallout of the economic logic was an increasing sense of disenchantment among agrarian communities, who believed that poor agricultural conditions were pushing them to the margins and started looking to the reservation policy to resolve it. This disenchantment led to the mobilisation of many dominant agrarian communities, who now demanded reservation in educational institutions and employment opportunities. The next section discusses these developments in detail.

Rethinking Debates on Representation

The 1980s were a decade of political upheavals due to the emergence of new social forces in the electoral–political scenario. It was a decade in which the demands of representation of various marginalised groups were consolidated. These demands were getting reflected in the electoral system in a more forceful way. This 'third electoral system', as Yogendra Yadav (1999) termed it, was of Bahujans, including women, Dalits, and the other backward castes. Yogendra Yadav noted how these groups were coming out and voting in large numbers in order to ensure that their voices were heard. During this period many regional centres of power emerged that were committed to advancing the cause of the backward classes. These were mainly agrarian castes who had a strong presence in the rural north Indian states.

The increasing participation of marginalised groups at various levels of policymaking eventually resulted in a collapse of status quo in the rural social order. The traditionally influential agrarian castes realised that their social status was changing. Increasing income diversification of young men and women coming from marginalised social groups generated a sense of frustration and having 'lost out' among the traditionally dominant social groups.

The new middle classes in India took a different form by the late 1990s and early 2000s. With a gradual rise in per capita income levels, a higher and stable economic growth rate, and relatively better human development index rankings in a few states, the new urban or semi-urban class was associated with increasing access to education and rapid urbanisation. This was particularly the case in areas which were the beneficiaries of Green Revolution of the 1960s on the one hand and the rise of sectors like services and tourism on the other. Punjab, Haryana, western Uttar Pradesh, parts of northern Karnataka, and southern Maharashtra can be placed in the first category. Central Karnataka and the present-day state of Telangana can be placed in the second category. Kerala, Gujarat, and the hilly areas of Himachal Pradesh and Uttarakhand can be placed in the third category.

Amid all these developmental currents, the landowning caste-class groups traditionally associated with agriculture, whose lands were getting smaller due to increasing family size, were the major stakeholders. Their access to education and exposure to a new urban lifestyle resulted in increasing aspirations for stability. Such stability became closely linked to having a secure job in the public sector.

With increasing costs of inputs in agriculture and declining profitability, a large number of agricultural households began to compete for government sector jobs. This provided the impetus for a new wave of political mobilisation. Consequently, Gujjars in Rajasthan, Jats in Haryana, Patidars in Gujarat and Marathas in Maharashtra launched extensive campaigns demanding reservation in government jobs.

The caste groups, owing to their numbers and dominance in the traditional social order, are highly influential and considered an important support base for political leaders. Hence, successive state and central governments have been under constant pressure to look for alternatives to include them in the policy for reservations. Reservation on economic grounds was one such available tool.

Reservation for Economically Weaker Sections

At a rally in Bihar that RSS Chief Mohan Bhagwat highlighted a need to rethink the policy of reservations. This statement created a nationwide uproar by Dalit groups and political resistance led by the opposition parties. BJP had lost the Bihar elections and it got only 53 seats out of 157 seats. Opposition leaders alleged that BJP's loss had a lot to do with its anti-reservation policy. Realising that this may harm the electoral fortune of BJP in Bihar, the BJP-led NDA government in 2019 declared that it had no such intention withdrawing reservations for the weaker sections. The Prime Minister in a statement reiterated that the government was committed to reservation policy (Rai 2015).

This statement had a political context. As discussed earlier, this period saw major agitations by dominant, non-OBC agrarian castes in all three states—Haryana, Maharashtra, and Gujarat—where the BJP had formed government at the state level, whether independently or as part of a coalition. The Patel agitations in Gujarat began in 2015 and there were reports of violence. In 2016, similar agitations occurred in Maharashtra where Maratha communities, under the banner of Maratha Kranti Morcha, demanded reservations for Marathas in government jobs. This agitation also turned violent. In 2016, Jats in Haryana also demanded reservation in the OBC category in the state. The increasing demands for quota within the existing reservation policy put both state and central governments under tremendous pressure.

A major political impact of these protests was that this created an environment of legitimacy for affirmative action policy across the political spectrum as the dominant social groups also started demanding quota within the existing affirmative action policy framework. Traditionally, the BJP, one of the major national-level parties, has consistently faced pressure from two of its core support groups—upper castes and corporates—to rethink the policy of reservations. The logic of merit has been supported by both these groups and they are against the affirmative action policy *in toto*.

However, the changing political landscape and BJP's rising support base among the backward classes and Scheduled Castes had forced the NDA alliance-led government to tread carefully on the issue of reservations. The concern about retaining its supporters among both backward and forward castes perhaps explains the NDA-II government's decision to expand the scope of reservations by bringing in an EWS quota. Through this new form of reservations, the government projected economic backwardness as a legitimate base for formulating quotas. Besides, presenting it as an alternative to caste-based affirmative action policy, the EWS reservation policy had provisions for opting any one kind of reservation i.e. either caste based reservation or economically backwardness based reservation. It was this clause that in effect made this quote exclusively for the upper castes.

The 103rd Amendment Bill, which created provisions for EWS reservations, was passed by both houses of Parliament through a voice vote, without any formal debate. While proposing the law, the government did not present any statistical findings on how the 10 per cent figure quota was decided—in contrast to the backward class reservations, which were backed by the recommendations of multiple parliamentary committess—nor did it specify how economic backwardness would be determined. Unlike discussions on inclusion or exclusion of castes in the reserved lists (in all three categories) where a commission is appointed or a proper legislative process followed, in this case no such procedure was followed.

Partha Chatterjee (2019) questioned the very idea of reservations for such a category. Chatterjee argued that social backwardness in the Indian Constitution is associated with backwardness of a group and not individuals. Thus, the prevalence of social prejudice and discrimination, and not economic status, were seen as markers of backwardness. If economic backwardness is taken as a criterion, is there a social group that qualifies for this?

In this context, this policy change is being seen as a threat to the constitutional idea of representation. It takes away the political logic of justice and discrimination and replaces it with a materialist understanding of reservation.

In its verdict on the constitutional validity of EWS reservations, the Supreme Court refused to put a stay on the policy. There was a division in the bench as two members did give their dissent note. The dissenting judges highlighted that the quota should not be seen as 'free pass' to the SC/ST communities. The dissenting opinion asserted that quotas were created 'only to offset fundamental, deep rooted generations of wrongs perpetrated on entire communities and castes'. It opined that the clause, which keeps backward classes and SC/STs out of the benefits of economic reservations, 'strikes a death knell to the equality and fraternal principle which permeates the equality code and non-discrimination principle' (Mandhani 2022).

Disinvestment and Reservations

A major policy shift that occurred as a result of the implementation of structural adjustment programme (SAP) was the state withdrawal from various economic activities especially manufacturing. During the 1950s and 1960s state in India invested extensively in heavy machinery manufacturing in order to create a base for industrialisation. Apart from facilitating industrialisation and providing employment, PSUs also had a social responsibility in the form of implementing reservation. It was in the year 1974 that an order issued by the Ministry of Home Affairs highlighted the provisions related to reservations in the Public Sector undertakings and voluntary organisations.[2] In the order the Ministry had only given an instruction highlighting that

> Autonomous bodies such as statutory and semi-government bodies which are under the control of the Government should also make reservations for Scheduled Castes and Scheduled Tribes in their services on the lines of the reservations in the services under Government vide instructions issued in Ministry of Home Affairs.

Besides, the provisions also gave exemption to scientific and technical posts from implementing reservations.[3]

However, with the process of disinvestment picking up pace the government gradually felt the need to relax some of its terms in order to attract investors. In a report published on *The Wire* it was highlighted that the 'Central government has informed potential private investors looking to take over state-run firms as part of its strategic disinvestment plan that they will not have to comply with quotas for reservation in employment' (*The Wire* 2022). The disinvestment plan took off during the late 1990s and later after 2014. What is further noteworthy is that on the one hand there have been hiccups in implementing reservations on the caste basis, most of the PSUs had shown a proactive interest in implementing the EWS reservation.

Although there are no specific reports available on the status of implementation of reservation in the public sector enterprises, in a recent report the parliamentary Committee on the Welfare of SCs/STs had highlighted that in case of PSUs the candidates appointed on reserved posts were being denied their dues by a delay in verification of caste certificates. The report was presented in the parliament. It was also highlighted that this was being used as a justification for delay in providing various financial benefits. So much so that there are employees who were at the verge of superannuation when they were informed that there caste certificate was not yet verified.

Summing Up

This chapter explained the debates on reservation policy in India which occurred in the aftermath of structural economic reforms. These debates were not merely about the economic issues associated with the policy of reservations as widely understood, but on larger questions about the changing nature of India's society and economy as well. The question of the rise of a new middle class within the communities identified as SC/ST and OBC was central to this debate. This was reflected in debates on the implementation of EWS reservations. As highlighted earlier, this has redefined the very idea of reservations by situating economic backwardness as the sole criteria to conceptualise reservations. The fundamental logic of untouchability (in the case of SCs) and social segregation (in the case of STs) has been ignored to prioritise economic backwardness.

Notes

1. Press release available at https://pib.gov.in/Pressreleaseshare.aspx?PRID=1783930 (accessed May 2024)

2. This order [O.M.No.27/12/73- Estt.SCT) dated 7/10/1974] is available at https://documents.doptcirculars.nic.in/D2/D02adm/Chapter-19.pdf (accessed May 2024).

3. Refer to the document available on the website of Lok Sabha. Available at https://persmin.gov.in/DOPT/Brochure_Reservation_SCSTBackward/Ch-02_2014.pdf (accessed May 2024).

Conclusion

This book has put forth a policy perspective on the issue of reservations that accounts for its different dimensions. As highlighted in the Introduction, reservation policy has emerged as one of the most contentious issues in Indian politics and policy discourse. The debate remains confined to three camps. One set of people believe that the very fact of reservation policy being based on caste or tribal status restricts its scope. They argue that instead of doing away with the caste, in actuality it further perpetuates caste segregation. Others defend caste-based quota as fundamental to the policy of reservations and positive discrimination, which in turn links to the question of representation. The third set of people demand certain modifications in the nature of reservations. Expansion of the policy, potentially to accommodate different dimensions of disadvantage, is one way of dealing with it.

In the arena of electoral politics, there has largely been a consensus in favour of a policy of reservations as it has provided space to various marginalised groups in the functioning of state machinery as well as politics. It has further democratised public institutions, leading to enhanced legitimacy and acceptance of various institutions and policies. Across the political spectrum, almost all political parties in India acknowledge the need to keep the reservation policy intact. However, the question of which groups should benefit and who should be kept out of its purview is still hotly contested.

As highlighted in the Introduction, the Constitutent Assembly was aware of this problem. B. R. Ambedkar, however, defended their decision to leave the term 'backwardness' open-ended, despite possibilities of litigation and other contestations, in order to bring different kinds of marginalised communities within the ambit of reservations. As highlighted in the Introduction, for Ambedkar, the idea of equality preceded backwardness as a principle of reservations. Equality constituted two major issues: untouchability in case of SCs and, physical segregation in case of STs. Backwardness and its forms were left open for the future governments to define without undermining the basic principle of social backwardness. The system of reservations based on backwardness was dynamic and not a settled debate.

However, transformations in electoral politics and the economy of India greatly influenced the trajectory of this ambitious policy intervention. By keeping the concept of backwardness open, perhaps the makers of the Constitution sought to ensure that the policy would not only correct the historical injustices of caste hierarchy but also address patterns of exclusion emerging in the future. Having a 10-year cap for political reservations in Parliament and state legislative assemblies reflects the optimism with which the Constituent Assembly viewed democracy and the future governments. However, they were well aware that due to entrenched structural inequalities and discrimination, attaining equity in the near future would be a difficult task.

The pace of implementation of reservation has been extremely slow and, in fact, in many ways a major political battle. This experience shows that policy implementation requires political support across parties. It was an outcome of a wider coalition of different socioeconomic groups, which resulted in a policy climate conducive to the implementation of reservations.

There are a few issues with regard to this policy that require the attention of not only policymakers or those tasked with implementation, but also academics and civil society at large. *First*, the issue of reservations must be seen in the context of the Constitution-makers' attempt to create truly representative public institutions. Reservations ensure that institutions are diverse in terms of socioeconomic, gender, and regional character and not merely a space controlled by a handful of individuals or groups. The idea of group-based representation is fundamental to this aim.

Second, merely having a reservation quota fulfilled does not ensure that discriminatory practices are eliminated. As shown in Chapter 3, various institutions that have been created for the purpose of facilitating reservations, such as SC/SC/OBC cells and the post of liaison officer, are stigmatised. There is a need for greater debate on how to handle discrimination and evolve dedicated institutional mechanisms to address it.

Third, a larger question remains unaddressed: Is representation a question that only public institutions should address? In a democratic polity, all institutions, whether public or private, have to be representative in character. It is the moral constitutional duty of a democratic state to ensure that this is realised in true spirit. However, so far, private organisations—companies, educational institutions, and the service sector—have been kept out of the ambit of this debate. This selective application of a logic of representation harms the foundational principles of the Indian Constitution: equality and fraternity.

This is a question that institutional theorists must ask: What are the moral foundational principles of an organisation or institution? Is it merely profit or do they bear a larger responsibility to the people? How far the issue of representation can be prioritised in light of this debate is critical to the idea of representation, reservation, or affirmative action; by making representativeness an optional criterion, the state shies away from its moral obligation.

The obvious question that follows this is how to achieve such institutions with a representative character. This is in line with the reservation debate, where usually the debate is: For how long? In our view, the answer is not complicated: 'Forever.' The question of equitable representation can scarcely become irrelevant in a democratic state.

Quite like how Ambedkar defended the logic of keeping backwardness open-ended, mechanisms for representation cannot and should not be based on fixed criteria. The existing cap of 50 per cent on reservations restricts the scope of the policy. Reservations must address a diverse range of variables including caste, class, ethnicity, gender, linguistic diversity, physical diversities, regional divide, etc. A multi-indicator index for such purpose must be created, and there is a need to go beyond an approach that hinges on a fixed percentage. Quite like the Human Development Index (HDI), the Indian state must work to develop a more holistic, all-encompassing set of criteria for defining backwardness and linking it with representation institutions and policies. A similar recommendation was made by the Sachar Committee in 2006 while looking into the status of minorities, especially Muslims, in India. The committee had recommended formation of an Equal Opportunity Commission to look into the grievances of deprived communities.

This book explicitly puts forward the idea that politics and policy go hand in hand and the two cannot be seen as separate. Politics cannot function without policy and without politics, policies have no essence. The reservation policy in India is the best example of this. The policy of affirmative action continues to remain voluntary as it gives priority to economic cost-benefit analysis over politics. A policy may be implemented effectively, and yet fail to produce desired outcomes, for instance empowerment of a population beyond certain statistics. Politics takes policies beyond statistics. In the Indian context, the reservation policy has not only achieved employment opportunities for the marginalised—this could have been achieved even with an affirmative action policy. Importantly, the reservation policy has also paved the way for mobilisation, collective assertion, and identity creation among marginalised communities across the political spectrum.

Yet, the larger challenge of proper implementation at the institutional level remains an issue. There is a need to bring in social auditing and monitoring of implementation of this policy at the micro level. Besides, people involved in enforcing such safeguards should be protected from any kind of harm, harassment, or intimidation so that they can perform their task freely. The three national commissions should be strengthened to ensure greater outreach. For this, special budgetary provisions are required. At the level of legislation, there is also a need to evolve a combination of mechanisms: incentives for achieving proportionate social representation and creating safe spaces, along with penalties for not implementing such provisions. Such measures should be applied not only to the public sector but also the private/voluntary sector.

A major initiative that has gradually come to a halt is the special component plan. The government must bring this plan back or bring in social budgeting to ensure representation in various institutions and organisations. Besides, there should be a special drive to ensure that marginalised groups are given priority in the implementation of various policies.

Above all, the Government of India must devise an all-India level policy framework for reservations. Such a framework will help destigmatise the idea of reservations, which is otherwise simply reduced to caste-based quotas with little regard for the rationale behind them. Caste is an integral part of the policy of reservation, but the spirit of reservations lies in the principle of proportionate representation and inclusion of all groups in the functioning of a democratic society. In order to build a framework that can spell out this objective and provide direction to future policy, it is essential to have a national-level committee to look into the status of the overall reservation policy and its implementation across central and state governments, in the public sector/autonomous organisations, and also in the private sector. A white paper should be placed before Parliament to understand the issues associated with a wider implementation of the policy of reservations.

References

Agarwal, R. C. 1998. *Constitutional Development and National Movement in India*. New Delhi: S. Chand and Co.

Ambedkar, B. R. 1979–2003. *Dr. Babasaheb Ambedkar: Collected Speeches and Writings*, volumes 1–17, compiled by Vasant Moon. Department of Education, Government of Maharashtra.

Ambedkar.org, n.d. *Jotirao Phule: Shetkaryaca Asud, Translated by Gail Omvedt and Bharat Patankar*. Available at http://www.ambedkar.org/gail/Phule.pdf (accessed May 2024).

Balagopal, K. 1990. 'This Anti-Mandal Mania'. *Economic and Political Weekly* 25 (40): 2231–2234.

Bertrand, Marianne, Rema Hanna, and Sendhil Mullainathan. 2010. 'Affirmative Action in Education: Evidence from Engineering College Admissions in India'. *Journal of Public Economics* 94 (1–2): 16–29.

Bhaskar, A. 2022. 'The Myth of the Ten-Year Limit on Reservations and Dr Ambedkar's Stance'. *Contemporary Voice of Dalit*. Available at https://doi.org/10.1177/2455328X221101674 (accessed May 2024).

Bhattacharya, Shrayana. 2021. *Desperately Seeking Shah Rukh: India's Lonely Young Women and the Search for Intimacy and Independence*. New Delhi: HarperCollins Publishers India.

Bose, Ajoy. 2009. *Behenji: A Political Biography of Mayawati*. New Delhi: Penguin Books.

Business Standard. 2018. '2015 Patidar Agitation: Gujarat Court Sends Hardik Patel to 2 Years in Jail'. *Business Standard*, 25 July. Available at https://www.business-standard.com/article/current-affairs/2015-patidar-agitation-gujarat-court-sends-hardik-patel-to-2-years-in-jail-118072500497_1.html (accessed May 2024).

Chandhoke, Neera. 2008. 'Three Myths about Reservation'. In Sukhadeo Thorat and Narender Kumar (eds), *In Search of Inclusive Policy: Addressing Graded Inequality*. Jaipur: Rawat Publications.

Chatterjee, Partha. 2019. 'The 10% Reservation is a Cynical Fraud on the Constitution'. *The Wire*, 18 January. Available at https://thewire.in/government/the-10-reservation-is-a-cynical-fraud-on-the-constitution (accessed July 2024).

Cochran, C. E., et al. 2003. *American Public Policy: An Introduction*. Boston, MA: Wadsworth/Thomson Learning.

Constituent Assembly debates. 1948. 'Constituent Assembly Debates on 30 November', Part 2, vol. 7. Available at https://indiankanoon.org/doc/75748/ (accessed August 2024).

———. 1949a. 'Constituent Assembly Debates on 26 August', Part 2, vol. 9. Available at https://indiankanoon.org/doc/707237/ (accessed May 2024).

———. 1949b. 'Constituent Assembly Debates on 14 October', Part 2, vol. 9. Available at https://indiankanoon.org/doc/54336/ (accessed May 2024).

Deshpande, Ashwini. 2013. *Affirmative Action in India*. New Delhi: Oxford University Press.

Deshpande, Ashwini and Thomas Weisskopf. 2014. 'Does Affirmative Action Reduce Productivity? A Case Study of the Indian Railways'. *World Development* 64: 169–180.

Deshpande, Satish and Yogendra Yadav. 2006. 'Redesigning Affirmative Action: Castes and Benefits in Higher Education'. *Economic and Political Weekly* 41 (24): 2419–2424.

Dushkin, L. 1979. 'Backward Class Benefits and Social Class in India, 1920–1970'. *Economic and Political Weekly* 14 (14): 661–667.

Economic Times. 2018. 'From Silent to Violent: The Journey of Maratha Quota Protests Mumbai', 25 July. Available at https://economictimes.indiatimes.com/news/politics-and-nation/from-silent-to-violent-the-journey-of-maratha-quota-protests-mumbai/articleshow/65135335.cms (accessed May 2024).

Economic Times. 2022. 'Gurjar Community Leader Kirori Singh Bainsla Dies', 7 April. Available at https://m.economictimes.com/news/india/gurjar-community-leader-kirori-singh-bainsla-dies/articleshow/90568360.cms (accessed May 2024).

Fernandes, Leela. 2006. *India's New Middle Class: Democratic Politics in an Era of Economic Reforms*. London: University of Minnesota Press.

Fuller, C. J. (ed.). 1996. *Caste Today*. New Delhi: Oxford University Press.

Galanter, Mark 1984. *Competing Equalities: Law and the Backward Classes in India*. New Delhi: Oxford University Press.

Gopal, P. G. 2021. 'Rethinking the Debate on Reservations'. *The Leaflet*, 16 August. Available at https://theleaflet.in/rethinking-the-debate-on-reservations (accessed May 2024).

Government of Tamil Nadu. 1971. *Report of the Backward Classes Commission, Tamilnadu*. Madras: Director of Stationary and Printing.

______. 1985. *Report of the Tamilnadu Second Backward Classes Commission*. Madras: Director of Stationary and Printing.

Gupta, Pallavi. 2012. *Backward Class Reservation and the Concept of Creamy Layer*. New Delhi: Deep and Deep Publications.

Jaffrelot, Christophe. 2003. *India's Silent Revolution: The Rise of Low Castes in Indian Politics*. Delhi: Permanent Black.

Jaffrelot, Christophe and A. Kalaiyarasan 2017. 'Quota is the Wrong Answer'. *The Indian Express*, 3 May. Available at https://indianexpress.com/article/opinion/columns/quota-is-the-wrong-answer-4637872/ (accessed May 2024).

Jain, Kalpana. 1990. 'A Myth the Muslim Created'. *The Indian Express*, 5 October.

Jayal, Niraja Gopal. 1997. 'The Governance Agenda: Making Democratic Development Dispensable'. *Economic and Political Weekly* 30 (8): 407–412.

Jodhka, Surinder S. and Katherine Newman. 2007. 'In the Name of Globalization: Meritocracy, Productivity and the Hidden Language of Caste'. *Economic and Political Weekly* 42 (41): 4125–4132.

Jodhka, Surinder S. and Aseem Prakash. 2016. *The Indian Middle Class*. New Delhi: Oxford University Press.

Joshi, Siddharth and Deepak Malghan. 2017. 'Faculty Diversity and Indian Institute of Management: A Preliminary Snapshot'. *Economic and Political Weekly* 52 (13): 12–14.

Keer, Dhananjoy. 1990. *Dr. Ambedkar: Life and Mission*. Bombay: Popular Prakashan.

Khan, Sarah. 2019. 'The Casteist Underbelly of Indian Private Sector'. *The Wire*, 15 March. Available at https://thewire.in/caste/the-casteist-underbelly-of-the-indian-private-sector (accessed May 2024).

Kohli, Atul. 1991. *Democracy and Discontent: India's Growing Crisis of Governability*. Cambridge: Cambridge University Press.

Kumar, Dharma. 1992. 'The Affirmative Action Debate in India'. *Asian Survey* 32 (3): 290–302.

Kumar, Narender. 2015. 'Mindset, Memoirs and Untouchability: Veracity beyond Conventional Structures'. In Vidhu Verma (ed.), *Unequal Worlds: Discrimination and Social Inequality in Modern India*. New Delhi: Oxford University Press.

LiveLaw. 2021. 'Narrow Concept Of "Merit" Allows Upper Caste Individuals To Mask Their Obvious Caste Privilege: Justice Chandrachud', 7 December. Available at https://www.livelaw.in/top-stories/justice-dy-chandrachud-caste-privilege-caste-discrimination-dr-ambedkar-187082?infinitescroll=1 (accessed May 2024).

Madhukalya, Amrita. 2021. 'Verify Caste Certificates within Six Months of Joining'. *Deccan Herald*, 16 December. Available at https://www.deccanherald.com/india/verify-caste-certificate-within-6-months-of-joining-parliamentary-panel-1061592.html (accessed May 2024).

Mahajan, Gurpreet and Surinder S. Jodhka. 2010. *Religion, Community and Development: Changing Contours of Politics and Policy in India*. London: Routledge India.

Mandhani, Apoorva. 2022. '"Fresh Injustice, Orwellian": Supreme Court Dissent in EWS Ruling Decries "Othering" of SC/STs, OBCs'. *The Print*, 8 November. Available at https://theprint.in/india/fresh-injustice-orwellian-supreme-court-dissent-in-ews-ruling-decries-othering-of-sc-sts-obcs/1203170/ (accessed May 2024).

Mendelsohn, Oliver and Marika Vicziany 1998. *The Untouchables: Subordination, Poverty and the State in Modern India*. Cambridge: Cambridge University Press.

Mishra, Dhiraj. 2020. 'Eye on Caste Vote Bank: Documents Show Modi Rushed 10% EWS Quota Law'. *The Wire*, 27 January. Available at https://thewire.in/government/ews-quota-consultation-law-ministry (accessed May 2024).

Mudaliar, Chandra. 'The Kohlapur Movement', PhD diss. Kohlapur: Shivaji Vidyapith.

National Commission for Scheduled Castes (NCSC). 2006. *Annual Report*. Available at ncsc.nic.in/files/ncsc/new88/292.pdf (accessed May 2024).

_____. 2010. *Fourth Annual Report*.

_____. 2016. *Ninth Annual Report*. Available at https://www.ncsc.nic.in/files/Combine_1.pdf (accessed August 2024).

National Commission for Scheduled Tribes (NCST). 2016. *Tenth Annual Report*.

Omvedt, Gail. 1994. *Reinventing Revolution. New Social Movements and the Socialist Tradition in India*. New York: Routledge.

Pai, Sudha. 2002. *Dalit Assertion and the Unfinished Democratic Revolution: The Bahujan Samaj Party in Uttar Pradesh*. New Delhi: Sage Publications.

Pandey, Neelam and Arnimesh Shankar. 2019. 'Reservation to Stay, Says Wary BJP as Mohan Bhagwat Raises Quota Bogey Before State Polls'. *The Print*, 19 August. Available at https://theprint.in/politics/reservation-to-stay-says-wary-bjp-as-mohan-bhagwat-raises-quota-bogey-before-state-polls/279044/ (accessed May 2024).

Penkar, Ahan. 2019. 'Why Teachers and Students are Protesting the 13-point Roster System for Faculty Recruitment'. *The Caravan*, 1 February. Available at https://caravanmagazine.in/policy/protests-against-thirteen-point-roster (accessed August 2024).

PRS Legislative Research. 2023. 'Women's Reservation Bill: The Issues to Consider'. *The Wire*, 20 September. Available at https://thewire.in/government/womens-reservation-bill-the-issues-to-consider (accessed August 2024).

R. Sujatha. 2020. 'UGC's Advisory on Reservations Roster Raises Questions on Implementation'. *The Hindu*, 27 October. Available at https://www.thehindu.com/news/national/tamil-nadu/ugcs-advisory-on-reservation-roster-raises-questions-on-implementation/article32947731.ece (accessed August 2024).

Rai, Siddhartha. 2015. 'RSS Chief Mohan Bhagwat's Comments on Reservation Policy Stirs Controversy'. *India Today*, 23 September. Available at https://www.indiatoday.in/mail-today/story/rss-chief-mohan-bhagwats-comments-on-reservation-policy-stirs-controversy-264144-2015-09-21 (accessed August 2024).

Rajan, A. 2019. 'Facts You Need to Know Before You Plunge into the Reservation Debate'. *Citizen Matters*, 18 January. Available at https://citizenmatters.in/facts-reservations-ews-sc-st-obc-government-court-9719 (accessed May 2024).

Ram, Anya Bharat and Gayatri Mann. 2019. 'Explainer: The Central Educational Institutions (Reservation in Teachers' Cadre) Bill, 2019'. *PRS Legislative Research*, July 3. Available at https://prsindia.org/theprsblog/explainer-the-central-educational-institutions-reservation-in-teachers%E2%80%99-cadre-bill-2019 (accessed August 2024).

Ramachandran, Aarthi. 2006. 'Parliament Panel Advocates Law for Affirmative Action'. *Economic Times*, 30 November. Available at https://m.economictimes.com/news/politics-and-nation/parliament-panel-advocates-law-for-affirmative-action/articleshow/644745.cms (accessed August 2024).

Ramaiah, A. 2008. 'Identifying Other Backward Classes'. In Thorat Sukhadeo and Narender Kumar (eds), *In Search of Inclusive Policy: Addressing Graded Inequality*. Jaipur: Rawat Publications.

Rao, Chinna Y. 2009. *Dividing Dalits: Writings on Sub-Categorization of Scheduled Castes*. Jaipur: Rawat Publications.

Report of the First Backward Classes Commission. 1955. Government of India.

Roy, Sandip. 2018. 'Harassment of Dalit Professor in IIT Kanpur Exemplifies the Subtle Ways of Caste Discrimination in India Today'. *Firstpost*, 4 April. Available at https://www.firstpost.com/india/harassment-of-dalit-professor-in-iit-kanpur-exemplifies-the-subtle-ways-of-caste-discrimination-in-india-today-4417983.html (accessed May 2024).

Sahai, Shambhavi. 2018. *The Relevance of Caste in Contemporary India: Reexamining the Affirmative Action Debate*, CMC Seminar Thesis (1854).

Saxena, H. S. 1981. *Safeguards for Scheduled Castes and Scheduled Tribes: Founding Fathers' Views*. New Delhi: Uppal Publishing House.

Shah, Ghanshyam, Harsh Mander, Sukhadeo Thorat, Satish Deshpande, and Amita Baviskar. 2006. *Untouchability in Rural India*. New Delhi: Sage Publications.

Sharma, Anupam Joya and Malavika Ambale Subramanyam. 2020. 'Psychological Response to Reservation-based Discrimination: A Qualitative Study of Socially Marginalized Youth at a Premier Indian University'. *International Journal of Educational Development* 79 (November). Available at https://www.sciencedirect.com/science/article/pii/S0738059320304570 (accessed May 2024).

Sharma, Harikishan. 2021. 'Amid Census Calls, Data Show Nearly Half of Rural Homes OBC'. *The Indian Express*, 29 September. Available at https://indianexpress.com/article/india/amid-census-calls-data-show-nearly-half-of-rural-homes-obc-7540637/ (accessed July 2024).

Sinha, Nidhi. 2015. 'Patel Agitation Turns Gujarat into a Battlefield'. *Mint*, 27 August. Available at https://www.livemint.com/Politics/bYe8fFBsGvJNJXpUmo9M3L/Patel-agitation-turns-Gujarat-into-a-battlefield.html (accessed May 2024).

Sinha, R. K. 1986. *Alienation among Scheduled Castes*. New Delhi: Manas Publications.

Srinivas, G. 2016. *Dalit Middle Class: Mobility, Identity and Politics of Caste*. Jaipur: Rawat Publications.

State of Working India. 2023. 'Social Identities and Labour Market Outcomes'. Centre for Sustainable Employment, Azim Premji University.

Subramanian, Ajantha. 2019. *The Caste of Merit: Engineering Education in India*. Cambridge, MA: Harvard University Press.

Suri, K. C. 1995. 'Competing Interests, Social Conflict and Politics of Caste Based Reservations in India'. *Nationalism and Ethnic Politics* 1 (2): 229–249.

Suthar, Sudhir Kumar. 2018. 'Bundelkhand Development Package, Drought and the Development Question in India'. *Social Change* 48 (3): 398–416.

The Hindu. 2015. 'Rajasthan Assembly Passes New Quota Bills', 23 September. Available at https://www.thehindu.com/news/national/other-states/rajasthan-assembly-passes-new-quota-bills/article7679698.ece (accessed May 2024).

———. 2021. 'Demand for Reservation Justified', 8 March. Available at https://www.thehindu.com/news/national/karnataka/demand-for-reservation-justified/article34015711.ece (accessed August 2024)

The Indian Express. 2023. 'SC Junks Pleas Challenging 10 per cent EWS Quota Ruling', 17 May. Available at https://indianexpress.com/article/india/sc-junks-10-per-cent-ews-quota-8613682/ (accessed August 2024).

The Times of India. 2018. 'Maharashtra Assembly Passes Bill Proposing 16% Quota for Marathas', 29 November. Available at https://timesofindia.indiatimes.com/india/maharashtra-govt-proposes-16-reservation-for-maratha-community/articleshow/66861960.cms (accessed May 2024).

———. 2021. 'Crimes Against SCs, STs in Rajasthan Saw Rise Compared to 2019 Figures', 17 September. Available at https://timesofindia.indiatimes.com/city/jaipur/crimes-against-scs-sts-in-rajasthan-saw-rise-compared-to-2019-figures/articleshow/86282971.cms (accessed August 2024).

The Wire. 2018. 'Maharashtra Assembly Passes Bill Proposing 16% Quota for Marathas', November 29. Available at https://thewire.in/government/maharashtra-govt-proposes-16-reservation-for-marathas (accessed August 2024).

———. 2021. 'Disinvesment: Won't Have to Comply With Reservation Quotas, Centre Tells Potential Investors'. *The Wire*, 31 March. Available at https://thewire.in/government/disinvestment-comply-reservation-quotas-centre-potential-investors (accessed August 2024).

Thimmaiah, G. 2005. 'Implications of Reservations in Private Sector'. *Economic and Political Weekly* 40(8): 745–750.

Thorat, Sukhadeo. 2004. 'On Reservation Policy for the Private Sector'. *Economic and Political Weekly* 39(25): 2560–2563.

Thorat, Sukhadeo, Aryama, and Prashant Negi (eds). 2005. *Reservation and Private Sector: Quest for Equal Opportunity and Growth*. Jaipur: Rawat Publications.

Thorat, Sukhadeo and Paul Attewell. 2007. 'The Legacy of Social Exclusion: A Correspondence Study of Job Discrimination in India'. *Economic and Political Weekly* 42(41): 4141–4145.

Thorat, Sukhadeo and Narender Kumar (eds). 2008. *In Search of Inclusive Policy: Addressing Graded Inequality*. Jaipur: Rawat Publications.

Viswanathan, S. 2009. 'Separate Slice'. *Frontline*, 16 January. Available at https://frontline.thehindu.com/social-issues/article30183414.ece (accessed May 2024).

Vox Populi. 2022. 'Caste in IIT Kanpur: Caste-based Social Realities That Shape Our Academic Existence', 1 May. Available at https://voxiitk.com/caste-in-iit-kanpur-caste-based-social-realities-that-shape-our-academic-existence/ (accessed May 2024).

Vundru, Raja Sekhar. 2003. 'The Quest for Equal Opportunity: Walking Through an Era of Reservation'. In *Hundred Years of Reservations: Appraisal and Assessment*. Hyderabad: 100 Years of Reservations Review Committee, Republican Party of Andhra Pradesh.

Weisskopf, Thomas E. 2004. *Affirmative Action in the United States and India: A Comparative Perspective*. London and New York: Routledge.

Yadav, Yogendra. 1999. 'Electoral Politics in the Times of Change: India's Third Electoral System 1989–99'. *Economic and Political Weekly* 34 (34): 2393–2399.